Charlie's Way:
Teacher and Pilot:
The Rest of the Story

Charles A. Magrady

PublishAmerica
Baltimore

First printing

PublishAmerica has allowed this work to remain exactly as the author intended, verbatim, without editorial input.

ISBN: 1-60703-770-X
PUBLISHED BY PUBLISHAMERICA, LLLP
www.publishamerica.com
Baltimore

Printed in the United States of America

I dedicate this little book to my wife, Lois,
the love of my life;
her help was always there when I needed it the most.

TABLE OF CONTENTS

Chapter One

Basic Training

It was April 12, 1943. And now it was my turn to report for duty in the U.S. Army by first visiting my local draft board on Ashland Avenue, where a small group of us draftees would assemble to begin our trek by train north to Fort Sheridan, Illinois. We had been inducted the week before in a simple ceremony in downtown Chicago that would reflect what was in store for us. When asked what branch of service I preferred and I answered "NAVY," the questioner promptly, and with great vigor, stamped my papers "ARMY!" And so my service began.

My poor Mother! It was very tough to bid her "goodbye." Since my Father, Charles Magrady, had died of lung cancer in November 1938, Ma depended upon her boys for emotional and financial support. Brother Bob, then the oldest, at 23, assumed head-of-family; brother Walter, 21, was not there to help. I would not be able to contribute to the family until I graduated from St. Philip High School in June 1940 at age seventeen.

Walter got me a job at Singer Sewing Machine Company on Jackson Blvd., where he worked, but then he enlisted in the Army for what he thought would be one-year service. The Japanese changed all that when they attacked Pearl Harbor, December 7, 1941; he was in for the duration. I stayed at Singer for fifteen months. I then went to work for Aladdin Radio Industries on 35th Street—near Sox Park, where I stayed until January 1943, when I was forced to leave for health reasons. The U.S. Army Ordinance Facility at 24th and Federal then hired me as a carpenter helper even though I was classified 1-A in the draft.

Across from the carpenter shop, where I worked most of the time, was a maintenance section, where women of all ages repaired starters, generators, fuel pumps, carburetors, speedometers, etc., for the Army jeeps and trucks that were being overhauled. The prettiest of these gals was a cute, little blonde that caught my eye. One lunch period, as I was perched upon a table outside the carpenter shop eating my bag lunch, I saw Lois looking my way (I knew her name because I checked her time card!). I motioned for her to come over to join me. When she came over to my table and sat down beside me, I almost flopped over!!

We finished our lunches in almost total silence—I was too shy and excited to talk—and I didn't know what to say, anyway.

Up close, Lois was even prettier than from afar. She lived in

Roseland, on Chicago's far south side. Just my luck to fall for a girl who lived half way to Indiana! After that first memorable meeting, we ate lunch together everyday and gradually overcame our shyness.

In due time, I summoned up enough courage to ask Lois to go out with me. When she said, "Yes," once again I almost fell off our lunch table!

That evening, I met her at the Illinois Central Station downtown and we went bowling at Benzengers. We had a fine time. Lois surprised me by her above-average bowling scores and I must say that I did pretty well, too. After bowling, we stopped in at Pixley and Eblers for a snack. Again we sat quietly with not much to say.

Later, I walked her back to the I.C. Station at Randolph so she could catch her train to Kensington 115th Street and home. I felt guilty about not taking her all the way home, but that was out of the question because it was so far and we had to work the next day.

And so my courtship of Lois Bross began. It was a classic case of "love at first sight," and then some! Our dates usually took place downtown with movies at the McVickers or Chicago Theater—or long walks along the lakefront bundled up against the wintry blasts. It's a wonder we weren't mugged! It was probably too cold for the crooks to be out! But you don't think of those things when you're young and foolish and in love!

At the beginning of February, I was shocked out of my state of romantic dreamland by the departure of my best friend, Joe Germanos, who was drafted into the Army and sent to the Aberdeen Proving Grounds in Maryland. Joe was the oldest child in a large close-knit Lebanese family and the emotional impact of leaving home for the first time almost drove him buggy. He told me later that during those first few weeks of basic training, he was so homesick that he almost went AWOL!

And my situation was similar to Joe's, and to many new recruits, I suppose, who had never been away from home and family ties before. It was especially difficult to say "goodbye" to Ma, knowing her worrying about how she was going to get along with caring for sister, Evie, who still had two years of high school and brother, Bill, who had just started to work.

Bill had been my sidekick and shadow for practically all my life (he was two years younger). When I pitched sixteen-inch softball, Bill was my catcher; when I practiced shooting goals in hockey, Bill was my goalie; we played one-on-one in basketball on our homemade court in our backyard (he was now taller than me and could out rebound me!)! How could I leave him?

The U.S. Army is not concerned about the condition of your heartstrings. I knew that, somehow, my family would survive whatever the WAR would send our way. And now I had Lois to worry about. She, too, I felt would be okay because she was strong and feisty and not weepy and wishy-washy. As we said our "goodbyes," we promised each other to be faithful and true, no matter what! We just had to wait and see how the Good Lord would help us along the way.

I don't remember much about the short train trip north from Chicago to Fort Sheridan. Brother Walter, after his enlistment and basic training at Fort Sheridan, worked there in the U.S. Army Reception Center. By the time I arrived at the Reception Center, April 12, 1943, Walter had left to attend the Infantry Officer's Candidates School at Fort Benning, Georgia.

This was our first taste of Army life. Our little group was formed into a larger group and then marched to a supply depot where we were issued most of our clothes and shoes and supplies that changed us into soldiers. Everything was brand-spanking new and fit pretty well considering the way we were issued the stuff. The supply soldier called out my shoe size as "Nine Charlie"—9C and I thought that was awful nice to have a shoe width named after me and I had just got there!

Wherever we were marched, other recruits, who had been there even a few days before us and could pick us out by our new spotless shoes, greeted us with a loud and boisterous: "YOU'LL BE SORRY!!"

On the second day at the Reception Center, because I loved airplanes so much and because I wanted to fly one way or another, I volunteered for the Paratroops. That same day, we were all given the Army's General Classification Test—their version of a general knowledge test. It was on the results of how well we did on this test, along with other criteria of past experience, that the Brass determined what to do with us.

I assumed that I had done pretty well on the AGCT when that same evening, a Major who worked in the testing section, called me in for an interview. After sizing me up—5 feet six, 135 pounds—he preceded to talk me out of volunteering for the Paratroops. He said that the Paratroops endured the roughest form of training in preparation for the most dangerous hand-to-hand combat. I figured that the Major knew more about it than I did, so I forgot about the Paratroops.

On the third day, I found out that I was assigned to the Air Corp for basic training and that we would be shipping out the next morning. I called Lois to tell her what I had learned and to say "Goodbye." That evening, after lights out and we were all tucked in our warm bunks, a loud speaker in our barracks called me to report immediately to the Visitor's Gate. Imagine my surprise when I arrived there, Lois and her mother had hurriedly traveled all across Chicago to the North Shore to bid me farewell!! What a wonderful surprise!!

Early the next morning, our troop train left Fort Sheridan and headed south.

None of us knew where we were going. Troop movements in wartime are top secret. Looking out the windows of our coach, gave us only a general direction of our travel. Slow going, to say the least.

That night we spotted a sign that informed us that we were

in St. Louis, Missouri. Right away, some guys thought we were headed for Fort Leonard Wood, MO—but that was not an Air Corp facility. Onward we rolled, south by southeast. A day passed, then another long night—sleeping sitting up in stiff coach chairs. Then another day greeted us with sunny skies and much warmer weather. The "Pecans for Sale" signs marked our march through Georgia! Soon we could see palm trees along the way and then we could be sure that we were headed south through Florida.

That evening, well after dark, our slow-moving train finally came to a screeching halt. Would this be it? Could we actually have reached the end of our journey?

Yes!! The order was given to leave the coach and to line up for assignment to trucks that would carry us to our final destination. A short ride of a few miles brought us into what seemed like a new and wonderful world seen only in the movies. As we left the trucks, bright moonlight revealed a long line of hotels that brilliantly rose skyward in all their glory. A soft ocean breeze warmly caressed our cheeks as we gazed in awe at this marvelous sight. And our new home was right there in front of us—Haddon Hall on beautiful Miami Beach!!

Haddon Hall was a swell-looking three-story hotel, shaped in the form of a "U." We were lined up and assigned our rooms by number. Did you ever carry a heavy barracks bag, loaded with everything you own in the world, up three flights of stairs? Grunts and groans and lots of profanity accompanied our ascent. After milling about in disarray, we finally located our room that would be home for the next five or six weeks. Six of us were assigned to a room that in usual circumstances would accommodate just two guests. Bunk beds and little else furnished our chamber. Not the Ritz, but who cares? It's better than a barracks, and besides, the wide-open windows bathed the whole room with balmy ocean air that beckoned your senses toward SLEEPYTOWN!

Reveille came early the next morning. We sleepily stumbled down the three flights of stairs and into the street (Collins Avenue) where we formed up into what they called "FLIGHTS." The uniform of the day was fatigues. Thank goodness, we finally had shed those heavy olive drabs (O.D.'s) that we had worn on our trip south. Each "flight" was made up of three squads of about ten men each; the tallest guys were put up front and the short fellows, like me, were lined up in the rear, with the medium-sized soldiers in the middle. That's a large part of my service marching experience—trying to keep up, and in step, with the big clowns up front!

A motley crew were we as we marched off to breakfast at a huge mess hall, which was located about three blocks away. This was our first real experience with standing in a chow line that crept with the speed of those huge Florida turtles. "Hurry up, and wait!"

The food was always good and worth waiting for: scrambled

eggs, toast, and sometimes French toast, or "S.O.S.—s___ on a shingle," greeted our starving stomachs.

After breakfast we were issued a very important item in our training equipment—a song sheet! Yes, a song sheet that had the words of all the many tunes we would learn to sing as we marched up and down Collins Avenue on Miami Beach. "Off we go, into the wild blue yonder, climbing high into the sun…" became our favorite song that filled our hearts with pride and wonder that we were actually part of this magnificent U.S. Army Air Corps!

The days were monotonous in their beauty—beautiful blue skies held sway every day. I remember that it rained only once the whole time I trained at Miami Beach. The weather was best in the morning and in the evening—in between those times, the sun beat down on us with merciless intensity, making the drill fields hot and steamy. You had to keep your exposed skin protected with oils and sunscreens. The non-coms charged with our training had to face that blistering sun every day so many of them covered their noses and tops of their ears with a white salve. Even so, sunburn was a huge problem.

Close order drill occupied most of our time. We had to learn how to march in step and how to execute various maneuvers on command. Gradually, with lots of practice and lots of patience on the part of our non-coms, we began to look like soldiers.

After several weeks of training, one afternoon we were standing "at attention," our Flight Leader Sgt. Wardlow looked down our column and saw that my left knee was sticking out a little when my legs should have been straight. With all the marching and drilling, an old basketball injury caused my left knee to swell. I didn't want to go on "sick call" because I didn't want to miss anything. The sergeant came down and took my name. That evening when my buddies were enjoying free time exploring Miami beaches, I was doing "extra duty"—marching up and down for two hours!

Getting shots in service was always a time you would like to forget—especially when they nailed you in both arms at the same time. That was enough to make you stand on tippy-toes! They usually had us line up in alphabetical order, so my roommate, Keith Lockwood, was always in front of me. Poor Keith's face would actually turn green as we waited our turn. He would almost pass out before and after getting stuck. I usually helped him through this ordeal by getting him to sit down for a couple of minutes. Somehow we managed, as we had no other choice.

Toward the end of our training, we fired the M-1 carbine rifle at 100 yards and 200 yards. I really enjoyed this time on the rifle range, but we never carried weapons elsewhere—not even on guard duty! About this time, there were rumors that a small German submarine was spotted off the coast of Florida. When my turn came to pull guard duty, I was assigned to walk a post up and down a stretch of the beach. Now at night, the darkness, with the waves rolling in and the wind making all sorts of strange noises, it was pretty scary. But I did have my Billy Club to protect me, and if the Germans attacked, I would whop them over the noggin with my trusty SHILLALAH!!

In the evenings and on Sundays, we had time to see a little of Miami Beach and to drink a lot of that delicious orange juice that was available everywhere. Writing letters home to Ma and Lois occupied much of what little free time I had.

"MAIL CALL" became the most important event in our lives as servicemen. We would flock around the non-com who brought the mail and he would call our names and hand the precious letters to us. When we got mail, our hearts raced madly in our chests; when there was nothing for us, dark clouds of gloom entered our souls. I was one of the lucky ones who received something almost everyday—either from Ma or from Lois. Ma wrote to Walter, too, to tell him that "poor Charlie" was "roughing it" in Miami Beach!

As our training droned on, all of us were deeply concerned about to what technical school we would be assigned. Flight crews overseas were taking a beating and needed replacements. Every bomber carried a pilot, co-pilot, navigator, and bombardier—all officers; the gunners in the B-17s and the B-24s came out of tech schools trained as radio men, mechanics, armorers, etc. Even though I wanted to fly in the worst way, my near-sightedness kept me out of flight school and I could not even qualify as a gunner. I feared the worst! I guess there was always COOKS & BAKERS SCHOOL—the catchall for misfits!

I soon learned that my fears were unfounded. My new assignment, one not considered even in my wildest dreams, would be at a college or university somewhere in the United States, as a student in the Army Specialized Training Program (ASTP). But first I had to report to the Citadel in Charleston, South Carolina.

The Citadel in Charleston, one of the oldest and most famous military schools in the South, had been taken over by the government to be used as a staging area for the Army Specialized Training Program. In June 1943, the way things were going in Europe and in the Pacific, it looked like this would be a long war. So the Army was sending the brightest of its recruits to colleges and universities all over the country for specialized training to prepare them for assignments wherever needed.

My first impression of the Citadel's building where we were assigned quarters was that of a dark, gloomy gray place which looked remarkably like a prison. The multi-tiered barracks building had many small rooms that opened out into the quadrangle. It was in one of these rooms that my life brightened up. My three roommates were all from New York City, and in the months to come, would all become my dear friends.

I don't know where their previous service had been, but Barney Luby, Marty Lefkovits, and Johnny Baird all joined me in giddy jubilation when we soon learned that we were headed north to New Haven, Connecticut and Yale University.

A wonderful assignment! Especially for my three new friends from the Bronx!!

Chapter Two
Yale University

When we arrived in New Haven, Connecticut, early in July 1943, even the cooler weather was cooperating in making our entrance to Yale a very pleasant event. We were assigned to Calhoun College, a very old and beautiful building on the very edge of the historic New Haven Green. A suite of rooms on the third floor became our new home.

Russ Harshman and I were given a small room that held a double bunk bed (Russ on top) and two desks and chairs. Here we would sleep and study in the months ahead. This room, in ordinary times, would occupy just one student. But we all thought that we had died and gone to heaven. As for me, I was tickled pink to have a chance to take some college classes, and at Yale University, at that!

Russ was about five feet eight inches tall and weighed about 180 pounds—a very husky young man. In civilian life, Russ had been a lineman for a power company in Salisbury, Maryland. He was a good athlete. So later on, he would collaborate with me on the touch football field and basketball court. But first, we looked forward to our class work in the Basic Engineering Program that the university had set up for the ASTP. I was extremely fortunate to have such a find young man as Russ as my roommate. My other new friends, Barney, Marty, and Johnny were located in rooms nearby on the same floor.

Even though we were now students at Yale and living in this grand Calhoun College, we were still in the U.S. Army. Reveille was at 6:00 A.M. when roll call was taken and the orders of the day were given. Breakfast followed in the beautiful dining room of the college where sumptuous meals were served by the regular food service staff in cafeteria-style—best food I ever ate!—and the long chow lines were a thing of the past. But still we were marched to our classes in regular army formations.

The Basic Engineering Program consisted of three 3-month trimesters. The curriculum was heavy with math, physics, and chemistry—especially loaded with college algebra and trigonometry classes that we attended six days a week—even on Saturday morning! Classes in English, History, and Geography rounded out our busy schedules.

Another important part of our program was our Physical Training. The University had set up a rigorous agenda for us in the gymnasium using the school's experienced staff. The leader of this group of torturers was a muscular young man who we promptly nicknamed "Supine Charlie" for most of our torso twisting exercises were done from the supine position. During the first week of our conditioning, we were tested to determine our general physical state and then, after four weeks of workouts three times a week, we were tested again, and those of us who scored above a certain level, were excused from the aches and pains in the gym and were allowed to participate in an outdoor touch football league. Wonderful!! (Barney, Johnny and I passed the test, but poor Marty was doomed to the gym for the duration!)

Each company of troops fielded several teams of six players. We played our games on lined-out fields eighty yards in length—forty yards wide, right next door to the Yale Bowl. To be outside, in pleasant weather and surroundings, playing a competitive but safe sport, like touch football, was extremely enjoyable. It helped us to take our minds off our schoolwork for a little while and to have some fun!

Throwing a football thirty or forty yards in tight spirals was one thing I was really good at. I became our team's quarterback and Russ Harshman and Johnny Baird became my favorite receivers. We won several games with our strong passing attack, which was well suited to this type of sport—mostly passing and not much running. However, when we played Company B for the championship, they beat us with a strong pass rush and better blocking. Thank You Lord for those splendid games of touch football!

Even with being almost totally absorbed in my studies and in my sports, I could not get my mind off of what was going on at home.

Lois' letters were not as frequent as in the beginning of my service, and what she wrote was troubling my soul. She began to question the soundness of our relationship—that we really didn't know each other that well, to begin with—that maybe our religious differences were too great to reconcile. What she wrote made a lot of sense, but when you're in love, who is sensible? I was afraid that I was losing her and one sad day, that letter arrived that confirmed my fears. It was a "Dear John" letter! Lois dumped me! My heart was crushed!

I let Russ read her letter and he promptly took her picture off my desk and put it in our wastebasket! I took her picture out of the basket and put it back on my desk. It was too much of a bitter pill to swallow all at once. It would take a little time for one to get used to the fact that I had lost the girl of my dreams.

It is at a time like this, in moments of great sadness, that we should turn to God for help. But I must admit that I didn't do this until, a few nights later, while sitting alone on a bench in the darkness of the New Haven Green, that I poured out my soul in anguish to the Lord. Why? Why? Please help me!!

I promised God, then and there, that if He would bring Lois back to me that I would do everything in my power to do His will in all things—that I would be a Model Christian. As things turned out later, He kept His part of the bargain, but, as for me, I failed miserably to keep my part. Lord Have Mercy!

One day, after our touch football season ended and we were working out in the gym, Russ and I were partners in learning a new Judo move whereby you grasped your opponent by the lapels, put your best foot in his gut, and rolled backward holding on with your hands and pushing with your foot and leg, tossing him into the air for surprising distances.

That evening, in our room, Russ was in a playful mood and began to wrestle me around and to tickle me in my ribs, as he sometimes was wont to do. Apparently, he had forgotten the Judo throws that we were doing earlier in the gym. He wouldn't stop bugging me so, without thinking, I grabbed him by his T-shirt, put my right foot in his gut, and rolled backward and tossed him. To my never-ending surprise, and I'm sure to his, he flew over my head, across the room, and crashed about half way up the opposite wall, fell down into a heap on the floor. I crawled over to him fearing that maybe I had hurt him seriously. But, Thank the Lord, he was not injured. By the way, Russ never tickled me again!

As we neared the last few weeks of our first trimester, I knew that I was in trouble as far as my grades in Math were concerned. I just barely passed college algebra (8 weeks) and trigonometry (4 weeks), even with Russ' expert help. I was doing fine in all my other class work. But I still had to face solid geometry and calculus down the line. I gave it my all and hoped for the best.

After our evening meal, we were locked in until around nine o'clock when the gates were opened for a short time so that we could go into the stores to buy necessities. Since there was no evening roll call, some of the boys would sneak out and gad about until the gates were opened at nine—or some would even stay out all night and slide into the area for reveille. Some of the windows on the first floor were left unlocked deliberately so that our "Pink Panthers" could get back in undetected.

I never did such "wild and crazy" things. The fear of getting caught and sacked was enough to keep me at my studies.

But once more, the evil hand of injustice slapped me alongside my noggin. Since my induction, I had never missed a formation, nor was I ever late for reveille. This one Friday morning I yelled "here" when my name was called at reveille. For some unknown reason, the company clerk marked me "absent." Our time was our own from noon Saturday until Sunday evening. So this Saturday, at noon, I was stunned to learn that because I had missed reveille on Friday, I was assigned "extra duty" for Saturday afternoon and all day Sunday. I was flabbergasted when they loaded me onto a truck with a bunch of "goof-offs" who had been caught sneaking in or out. They drove us out to a nearby woods to chop trees and do other cleanup work.

It was sunny and pleasant in the woods so I really didn't

mind very much. While Barney, Marty, and Johnny were having a great time at home in NYC, here I was doing "extra duty" for something I didn't do. But in the long run, the Brass did me a favor, they didn't punish me by sending me into the woods to work because I enjoyed the outing immensely!

My New York friends went home almost every weekend. Barney Luby was a chubby Irishman about my size who exhibited Falstaffian characteristics—he was fun loving and jovial. He didn't walk—he bounced along always with a grin or smile on his kisser. He loved to exercise his tenor voice with the latest hit songs from the New York stage. On one of his trips home, he went to see the new musical "Oklahoma," and, of course, you could hear him singing "People Will Say We're in Love," all over Calhoun College!

And Barney loved to dance. He couldn't wait to get home to the Bronx for that Saturday night dance with some pretty girl. He could "Lindy" all night long and some Saturday nights, he did!!

Marty Lefkovits also went home almost every weekend, but his activities were not like Barney's. Marty lived a quiet life with his widowed mother. He was taller than me and he wore glasses. Marty was soft spoken and studious and had a great sense of humor. While he laughed at our jokes and nonsense, he was always ready to listen to our problems and help us out anyway he could. One weekend, Marty took me home with him to meet his mother and to show me around Manhattan. A wonderful visit!

Johnny Baird was a wiry Irishman about my size—quiet and laid-back. To look at him, you would never suspect that he had recently won the featherweight boxing championship of the U.S. Army in Texas.

Jack, one of our boys at the Yale Gym made the mistake of underestimating Johnny's boxing prowess. This guy was six inches taller and outweighed Johnny by at least thirty pounds. He wanted John to give him a boxing lesson and he wouldn't take "no" for an answer. Finally, Johnny gave in and the two gladiators climbed into the ring wearing those large 12 oz. training gloves.

They sparred around awhile, feinting and dancing, landing light blows, bobbing and weaving. Then John began to hit Jack with his lightning fast jabs—nothing really hard but just enough to show Jack what superior speed and experience can mean in the ring. With every stinging blow, I could see that Jack was getting more furious every second. Then, in a flash, after another sharp jab to his whiskers, Jack flew into a monstrous rage as he chased Johnny around the ring, swinging wildly as hard as he could. His footwork and skill in blocking punches kept John out of trouble. He knew the overheated young man needed to be cooled off so he stepped inside of one of Jack's haymakers and delivered a stunning right cross that buckled

Jack's knees and sent him crashing to the canvas. No harm done, but a lesson well taught!

Not too long after that exciting boxing demonstration and my "Week-End in the Woods," events unfolded that helped to relieve my aching heart.

On May 20, 1943, Brother Bob married his sweetheart Millie Deluise at St. Jarlath's. Soon after, he was drafted and sent to Camp Lee, Virginia for basic training. Meanwhile, my ole buddy Joe Germanos had completed his basic training at Aberdeen Proving Grounds in Maryland. Somehow, Lady Luck smiled on us for through our correspondence; we were all able to get weekend passes and to make it into New York City for a marvelous get-together. Even though we were only able to visit for a few hours on Sunday, it was a good taste of home and family.

The second trimester began on October 11, 1943. The course work was pretty much the same as the first trimester—heavy on math and physics and chemistry. I did well in all subjects again—except math (solid geometry). No matter how hard I tried and despite much help from my roommates, I was failing math miserably. But there were other compensations in the sport field.

After our touch football season ended (we lost the championship game), it was announced that there would be tryouts for the company basketball team. I loved basketball, so when the time came to show what we could do, I was right there with "Great Expectations."

We were divided up into two teams with the coaches, armed with clipboards and whistles, on the sidelines. I played guard and brought the ball down the floor with another lad who hailed from Kentucky. Once again the Good Lord smiled on me for, even though the scrimmage was short, it so happened that every shot I took went in! I hit the basket from every spot on the floor—left handed, right handed, set shots—I couldn't miss! It was an incredible experience and on the basis of our performances, my teammate from Kentucky and I were chosen co-captains of our company team. Afterward, another player remarked, "You really had "Hot Pants" tonight!"

Our basketball league lasted throughout the fall until almost Christmas when, once again, we played for the championship—and lost! But Thank You, Lord for all those great games in the Yale gym!

At Christmas time we were given a ten-day furlough and, of course, I headed for home. As the train neared Chicago, I got the strangest feeling, looking out of the window at the names of places that were so dear to my heart. This is Chicago—my Chicago, my hometown! For the first time, I realized just how much I loved this town and how much I missed this town. And on subsequent visits home my heart always beat faster as I got close to the city and the family that I loved so much. While Florida was beautiful, New Haven was historic, and New York

City was imposing, Chicago and its West Side would always be the only place for me!

It was so wonderful to greet Ma with hugs and kisses and to wrestle Bill around again, and to laugh and joke with Evie and Irene. They all thought that I looked great in my uniform—Buck Private—with a few added pounds from that delicious food from the Yale kitchen!

The days at home were passing quickly. The joy in my heart was tempered by the cold reality that I had not heard from Lois in several weeks; I didn't call her and she didn't call me. What to do? I decided that I would take my beloved figure skates downtown to the Chicago Arena for an afternoon of ice-skating.

The Chicago Arena, which I had visited several times before being drafted, was a really swell place to skate. It was the home of the Chicago Figure Skating Club that I had hoped to join so that I could take some lessons. I had dreams of learning to skate well enough so that I could try out for a line job in the ice shows that came to town every year. But Uncle Sam had different plans for my future.

That Saturday afternoon, while cavorting around the ice, I set my radar on a pretty young girl with long auburn tresses. She could skate okay so I asked her to join me in a few spins around the ice. She agreed, so began another adventure.

Her name was Pat and she lived in Glencoe up on the North Shore. She was still in high school and had come down to the

Arena because she loved to skate. We got along really well from the very start and spent the rest of the afternoon together, making turns around the ice, visiting the skate shop, and just sitting and talking. When it came time for us to part, Pat invited me to her home the next evening for dinner and to meet her family.

I was honored to accept her invitation and arrived ahead of the appointed time. Her beautiful home and the neighborhood in which she lived in Glencoe gave one the feeling that this place was long established in well-earned, authentic wealth. I met her father and mother and younger brother and we were all soon seated around a lovely dining table in a lovely dining room.

Pat's family proved to be as warm and friendly as she was. They did their best to make me feel "at home," but I had trouble getting over my innate shyness. They seemed to be quite impressed when they learned that I was home on leave from classes at Yale University.

After dinner, mother, father, and brother put on their coats and departed for the local movie house. A marvelous display of trust—trust in me, and trust in their daughter—to leave us alone for awhile. Then Pat sat down at their grand piano and began to play, play really well—mostly popular tunes. I stood by the piano, just like they do in the movies, and there, to my astonishment, Pat looked deeply into my eyes and began to sing a love song to me! Here I was, a guy who got nervous and shaky even when a girl spoke to me and at this moment a very pretty girl is serenading me like Jeannette MacDonald did to Nelson Eddy! Only I was no Nelson Eddy! All I could do was to smile, and listen, and hope that I didn't faint!

When the song ended, we kissed—just like they do in the movies—and then the magical moment was over.

Pat explained that she had been developing her musical talents for the past several years and that she, on occasion, played and sang for the sailors up at the Great Lakes Naval Training Station, and for other gatherings of service men and women.

Time waits for no man, so I had to thank Pat for a swell dinner and the musical treats that followed, and to hustle to the station to catch my train back to reality! On the ride home, I pondered over in my mind the events of the past few hours and I decided not to pursue this relationship any further.

Pat was a beautiful, talented, wealthy young lady who undoubtedly had a great future in store; I, au contraire, was a plain, poor boy from the West Side whose future was cloudy, to say the least. I had nothing to offer her, so I let the whole thing dissolve into thin air. Besides, I still loved Lois!!

Chapter Three
On to Madison

Back at Yale, the second trimester ended with the coming of the New Year. I passed everything except Math. Lieutenant Kinnard, who was in charge of our company, called me in and gave me the sad news that because of my failing grade in Math, I was being dropped from the program and would soon be given another assignment. For the next few weeks I would still be able to attend classes while my new orders were being processed.

Of course, I was depressed over this latest development, but I felt that I had given it my best shot, which simply wasn't good enough. What would they do with me next? Trust in the Lord!!

In due course, my orders came through and I was being shipped back to the Air Force in Greensboro, NC for reassignment. I departed Calhoun College, which I had grown so fond of in just six months, on a cold Saturday afternoon in

February for the New Haven Railroad Station. Barney, Marty, Johnny, and Russ all helped me lug my two barracks bags to the station. It was really tough to say "Goodbye" to these dear friends who had become an important part of my life. I never saw any of them ever again! A sad farewell!

The Air Force installation at Greensboro, North Carolina was very large and many faceted. We called it a "repo depot" because here the Air Force collected men from all over the United States and even overseas into large pools, which awaited reassignment. Part of the camp was involved in Basic Training activities where new inductees and some guys, like me, who were not so new in the Army, were mingled together. It was here that I had to bide my time while the slow wheels of planning crept forward. I thought it demeaning that I had to take Basic Training again, but I soon had a new perspective.

My comrades in the barracks were not new recruits—quite the opposite. These men were all "Buck" Sergeants, Staff Sergeants, Tech Sergeants—all aircrew members who had flown their required twenty-five missions in combat in Europe and had been returned home to the States for reassignment or discharge. Needless to say, they were all so happy to be safe and sound on the ground in Greensboro, instead of being shot at by Folke Wulfs or blown up by enemy flack!

When I saw how graciously they underwent the nonsense of retraining, listening to military lectures, sitting outside in the cold dampness of North Carolina, I changed my attitude. I now considered it an honor and privilege to be with these heroes who had risked their very lives in B-17s and B-24s over Europe to protect our freedoms here at home.

They, who had suffered with the bitter cold in the bombers at high altitude over Europe, were now trying to keep warm on the ground in North Carolina. I shivered along with them even though I had on my "Long Johns," woolen O.D.'s, field jacket, and long woolen overcoat! I was glad to leave North Carolina so that I could warm up!

After a long wait of four weeks, my orders finally came through, and I was on my way, not overseas, as I had expected, but to Radio Mechanic School at Madison, Wisconsin! Imagine my joy when I learned that I would be staying in the Air Force at Truax Field for the next six months, at least! And only 150 miles from home!!

On the long train ride from Greensboro to Madison, with a change of trains in Chicago, I was not traveling alone, but with a young airman who hailed from New Bedford, Massachusetts. I was very happy that I was going much closer to home, but my new friend, Rodger Perkins, was sad that he was going farther away from his beloved Boston Red Sox and his idol, Ted Williams!

Rodger was a slim, sandy-haired youth, nineteen years old, who loved baseball with a passion. He was shy and soft spoken, but when I informed him of my great love for sports, in general, and baseball, in particular, he opened up and by the time we reached Madison, Rodger and I were already good friends. He, later on, would be best man at my wedding!!

When we reached Truax Field, it was still winter in Wisconsin, but while the temperature hovered in the low teens, it did not feel nearly as frigid as it did in North Carolina. And when we were given a few hours off duty, a local bus took us into downtown Madison, the capital of Wisconsin. We walked around the Capitol Building and checked out the stores and restaurants on the square. Rodger and I liked what we saw and were very optimistic about our new assignment.

In a few days, our schooling began in large special buildings a few blocks from our barracks. The classes were small—about twelve men in a group—with army instructors. Every Air Force airplane was equipped with radios that needed servicing and that was our new job—to learn all about the equipment—how to install it and how to keep it running in tip-top shape. So for six hours a day, five days a week, we studied radio theory and practice.

Physical training occupied part of our schedule every day, and Rodger and I were pleased to know that tryouts for our Flight's softball team would be held as soon as weather permitted. This would be 12-inch fast-pitch softball—kind of a mix between regular hardball and 16-inch softball.

Meanwhile, we attended classes during the week and, on weekends, we sometimes were given 16-hour passes so we could leave the field and travel where we pleased. Of course, the first chance I got I went home to Chicago.

Ma, and Bill, and Evie, and Irene were all so happy to see me. I was thrilled to be home, too, even for such a short visit, because I knew that this was just the first of many visits that I would make in the weeks and months to come.

My joy was not complete though because, in the back of my mind, I always thought of Lois and how much I missed her, and how great it would be to see her again. I didn't discuss this with Ma or the rest of the family because I found out that sometime during my basic training, Lois and her mother came over to our house for a visit, probably to check us out. As I later surmised, Ma was not impressed with them, and Mrs. Bross and Lois were somewhat displeased with Ma and our dilapidated homestead.

Despite this gloomy outlook, on a subsequent visit home, I called Lois and, to my astonishment, she agreed to see me again. She seemed pleased that I was now stationed close to home and that we could see each other, if only on weekends. But her opposition to a serious relationship with me was still very much in evidence. She was against me, and so was Ma! I had to get to work! God Help Me!!

Chapter Four
I Seize the Pearl

In the weeks that followed, I was beginning to feel alive again. Spring was in the air! Everyday was a little bit warmer, and softball tryouts were in the offing. Our radio classes were informal and extremely interesting. I always liked science so learning something new was exciting and challenging.

St. Patrick's Day was upon us, so, of course, we had to enjoy an Irish joke:

> *In the days long past, it was customary*
> *To wake the deceased at home, usually,*
> *in the front parlor. Well, O'Brien came*
> *by to pay his respects to his departed*
> *friend, O'Toole. After kneeling at the*
> *bier for a few moments, he consoled the*
> *widow, "He looks so natural, Mrs. O'Toole*

and when I touched his hand, it felt warm!"
Without batting an eye, Mrs. O'Toole replied,
"Hot or cold, he goes out in the morning!"

It was not always a sure thing to get a pass on my day off, but when I did, I always went home to see Lois and my family. After a few visits, it became clear to Ma that I was spending more and more time with Lois, and less time with her. Ma didn't have much formal schooling, but she knew her sons and daughters quite well, and she could read me like an open book. And what she saw she didn't like and she told me so.

"Charlie," she said, "this girl is not the one for you."

"But, Ma," I replied, "I love Lois and I want to marry her!" To which Ma gave me an ultimatum.

"If you marry her, don't come home!!" Wow!! What a slap in the kisser!

Of course, when Lois asked me how Ma felt about us seeing each other so much, I lied to her and said that Ma had no objections to our relationship. I wanted her at all costs—even to sacrificing my own integrity. When lies and deception came in the door, wisdom went out the window!

So after a whirlwind courtship in the early months of summer 1944, Lois agreed to become my wife. We were married in the Chapel at Truax Field on August 10, 1944. Ten of my army buddies attended the Saturday afternoon affair and Rodger Perkins was my best man. Ruth Lindborg, Lois' best friend, was her maid-of-honor. Lois' parents, Fred and Louise Bross, approved of our nuptials but wondered why they were not invited to the wedding.

Ma found out about it when Father O'Brien at St. Jarlath's mentioned my request for my baptismal certificate so that the Chaplain at Truax would marry us.

After the ceremony, the four of us—Lois and I, Rodger and Ruth—went out for our wedding supper—a simple affair in a Madison restaurant. When I thought about it later, I had a lot of nerve marrying this wonderful girl when I had absolutely nothing to offer her—she even had to lend me the money to pay for our wedding bands!

We spent our honeymoon in a Madison hotel that Sunday and when I returned to camp the next morning, I had to use a Class A Pass that one of my buddies, Private Hunt, let me borrow. Unfortunately, I was a little late signing in Monday morning and the Second Lieutenant in charge confiscated the pass. He later called Private Hunt down to the Orderly Room and when he saw that it was not I, but Private Hunt, the Lieutenant began a search for ME!! I was extremely lucky—a few inspections were hairy, but he never found me!!

But, as I said, Ma found out about us and threw a fit! And she wasn't the only one. Brother Bob, upon learning of our wedding, sent me a nasty letter in which he lambasted me for abdicating my family responsibilities! But in a short while, they both got over their rancor and Ma wrote, "Come home, Charlie, and bring you new bride with you!!"

With that invitation in mind, and suspecting that tempers had cooled, on one of my subsequent passes from the field, I took Lois to visit Ma and Bill and Evie, and Irene and her bunch who lived next door. They all liked Lois from the start and she liked them; it was the beginning of a solid family relationship that lasted through the many years to follow.

They say "Time passes quickly when you're having fun!" and the six months at Truax Field whizzed by in a flash with my courtship and marriage to Lois, my great visits to my home and to hers, my acceptable performance in Radio Mechanics School, and those fantastic games on the softball field.

Now it was time to move on to the next phase of our training, which was a four-week program on radio antennas at Chanute Field, Rantoul, Illinois. The Illinois Central Railroad passed right through Rantoul; so after finishing my work for the week, I could hop on a late night train for Chicago, get the conductor to stop the train at Kensington (115th St.), walk up the hill and to the Bross residence, climb the stairs to the second floor, enter quietly through the kitchen door which had been left open for me, and then like a kitten with softly padded feet steal into Lois' bedroom and into her warm and waiting arms. It was so good to be home!!!

It was so good, in fact, that these wonderful visits led me to make a dumb decision that I would later regret—I purposely failed the practical test that they gave us at the end of the week's work so that I would be able to get home one more time. Foolish boy!! I had to repeat that week's work—now with a different group of students. My original class finished their work at Chanute Field and shipped out for Boca Raton, Florida. My buddy, Rodger Perkins, could no longer be my sidekick. I was so sad to see him go and I know he felt the same way. He was a caring and sensitive lad who knew that people in love do crazy things!

Eventually, I completed the course at Chanute and was promoted to the rank of Corporal. The next stop, at the end of a two-day train ride, was the airfield at Boca Raton, Florida. Here we would work on the actual radios used mostly in B-25s and B-26s—medium bombers.

Leaving Lois was very difficult—I hated "Goodbyes." But our separation would not be for long. I soon received the happy news that married non-coms (like me!) could live off the post with a Class A pass—as long as we attended all our formations and class work on time. Within a week or so, I lined up my Class A pass, checked the available living accommodations near the Field and found a suitable room with a couple in Lake Worth. I called Lois and told her to "come on down!"

The Franklins were an elderly couple that had come down to Florida for health reasons from Cleveland, Ohio. Their bungalow was small, yet they provided us with a nice sleeping room for $30 per month. My pay at that time was $50 per month, so you can see that we had to watch every nickel. We had no kitchen privileges; Lois had to eat all her meals out. I ate breakfast and lunch at the Field and joined Lois in the late afternoon for our evening meal. Luckily, a nearby restaurant provided good food at reasonable prices. Also, Lois and I were not big eaters, so we managed the food problem quite well.

Living off the field dictated my getting up at 3:30 A.M. to catch the 4:00 A.M. bus for Boca Raton. We arrived at camp in time to join the other troops for reveille, and then breakfast, followed by physical training composed of calisthenics and a lot of long runs in the sandy soil. During the rest of the morning and all afternoon we worked on aircraft radios. Around 4 P.M., we were through for the day and I headed home to Lake Worth and Lois. Through experimentation, I found that the quickest way to cover the 20 miles to Lake Worth was not to go out the main gate of the Field, then to wait for a bus going north, but to take a shortcut through the brush along a path that led to a low fence that marked the edge of the Field. The main highway was right there and I usually managed to get a ride from someone driving north.

One of the B-26 pilots from the Field frequently was going home about the same time I was, so he was kind enough to let me ride behind him on his motorcycle. Needless to say, I enjoyed these fantastic trips more than all the rest!

Taking these shortcuts through the brush was, at times, a little scary. You had to be careful not to step on a coral snake or a scorpion. One afternoon, as I rounded a bend in the narrow path, a huge turtle with a head as big as a basketball sat right smack-dab in my way. I thought it was over, and then decided to speed around him as fast as I could go. He didn't move a muscle as I flashed past him at top speed. As far as I know, he may still be there.

Because we radio mechanics were part of the Air Force, our superiors decided that our physical training should include Parachute Landing Training. This didn't bother me because I loved everything about airplanes, but some of the boys were not too thrilled about this new adventure.

They started us off by having us jump off a wooden platform about six feet above the ground. When we hit the ground, we were supposed to tuck our heads to the side, bend our knees, and *roll* head-over-heels. This took some practice! Then we had to learn how to wear the parachute harness and to jump off the platform holding the risers to the chute. No matter what happened, you NEVER let go of the risers!!

Next came the fun part! They had this huge apparatus that had a fifty-foot tower at one end and a slanted cable from the top of this tower about a hundred feet or so to a low post at the other end which was about ten feet above a sand pit. We would climb up the stairs to the high end of the cable where our parachute harness was hooked on to a free-running pulley, step off the platform and slide down this cable—building up speed as we went. An instructor had control of our harness attachment as we rolled down. When we reached a point over the sand pit at the low end, he tripped our harness loose so that we fell into the sand below. We were supposed to tuck and roll just as we did off the wooden platform. And, of course, as we came down and hit the ground, you *NEVER* let loose of your risers!

My first trip down the wire was a disaster! As I slid down the cable, I thought, "Gee, this is like Riverview." I even remembered to hold my risers tightly in my fists. But when he dropped me into the pit, I didn't roll the way I was taught, but, instead, I buried my head in the sand! I can still hear that Second Lieutenant as he stood over me and shouted in my ears "Fifty Pushups!!"

With that kind of encouragement, my next trips down the wire were much better. By the end of the week's training with many landings performed, we were pretty good at controlling how we hit the ground. The instructors told us that now that we were experts, we could come out to the airfield on Saturday and jump for real out of a C-47. I don't think any of my group accepted the offer! I know I didn't!!

While my military training was going forward without any serious problems, and while Lois and I were getting to know each other better with each passing day, both older brothers, Bob and Walter, were now giving their lives to U.S. Army service. Now all three of us were married men—Bob, Millie and Walter, Mary. Walter was a Second Lieutenant in the 81st Wildcat Division which had gone to the Pacific Theater, and

Bob—even though he came into service after I did—after a few short months of basic training—was already running a Postal Unit in combat in Europe!

Meanwhile, I was fighting the war at Boca Raton. From the very beginning of my military service, I was determined to give it my very best effort—no matter what the assignment. Now that I had Lois to support, I started to think about how I could improve our bleak financial picture. The government was already taking part of my pay to send home to my Mother. With my promotion to corporal, I received a small increase. It was then that I learned that Second Lieutenants made $175 per month. Wow!!

I went down to the Personnel Section and inquired about what opportunities were available in Officer's Candidate Schools. Only a few schools were open—Infantry (of course!), Engineers, Supply, and Motor Pool. Which of these was I suited for—if any? The wheels in my head began to whirl!

Several weeks passed, then several months. Spending the Christmas season here in sunny Florida was really different. For entertainment, Lois and I managed to take in a movie, once in a while, up at West Palm Beach. What we really enjoyed most was going to the wild-and-wooly wrestling matches held in a local Lake Worth arena. We knew the matches were fake and "put-ons" and not for real. Some of the wrestlers and their managers ate their supper in the same café that we did and we could hear them planning the "script" for that night's bouts!

But it was great fun to see and hear how involved some of the audience became. One fat, boisterous lady, who always seemed to sit near us, would lose her cool and end up screaming obscenities at the "villains" in the ring! It was fun because, in spite of all the yelling and screaming, no one got hurt!

Rodger Perkins would come to visit us on his free days. It was really nice to see him again and to pal around together just like we used to do up in Madison. Lois spent a lot of time each day at the beach, which didn't cost anything and was within walking distance. She soon had a great tan! On weekends, the American Legion Hall that was directly across the street from our house, held dances and the music could be heard for blocks around. It was a small band that featured a saxophone pealing the plaintive plea "Don't Fence Me In!" We heard that tune even in our dreams! But we were happy and content with our situation. Little did we know that our dreams would very soon quickly turn into nightmares!

Chapter Five
Goodbye, Billy!

Late In January 1945, on a beautiful warm and sunny Sunday morning, Lois and I were enjoying a few extra winks when the doorbell rang. Mr. Franklin answered the door and called me to come to sign for a telegram that the Western Union courier held in his hand. I checked the name and, sure enough, it was for me. When I opened the telegram and read it, I could not believe my eyes. It read, "CHARLIE, BILL DIED LAST NIGHT, FUNERAL TUESDAY. RED CROSS WILL CONFIRM. IRENE."

What is this? I couldn't believe this. I read it again, and again! I looked away, and then read it again. My brain was having trouble understanding the message that my eyes beheld! Lois took the piece of paper out of my hand and when she read it, she began to cry. I could not cry for I was in a state of shock!

How could this be true? I didn't even know that Bill was

sick. Ma's last letter, a few days before, said that he was having headaches—but nothing serious. He had been working everyday without any sign of illness.

Of course, I had to get home as fast as possible to comfort my poor mother, and Irene, and especially Evie who was so close to Bill.

Lois and I made it to the Field and began a wait that would turn me sour on the Red Cross for years to come. Headquarters issued my emergency furlough promptly but told me that I could not leave the Field until the Red Cross confirmed my brother's death. We waited hours—an agonizing wait until the confirmation finally came through.

We took a bus to Miami because we were told that my best chance of getting a free ride north in an Army airplane would leave out of Miami. No planes were bound for Chicago, but there was a C-46 leaving for Detroit, Michigan. I figured that I could fly to Detroit, and then hop a train for Chicago—about a six-hour ride. Of course, Lois could not go aboard the military flight and I kissed her "goodbye" and hoped that some how she could follow me hours later. What happened next turned out to be the four most terrible days of my whole life!

Our airplane took off Monday morning about 10 A.M. in lovely 80° weather. There were about a dozen other Air Force personnel aboard "bumming a ride" just as I was. The C-46 was mostly a cargo plane with bucket seats along both sides of the fuselage. That's where the paratroopers sit before they bail out. It was comfortable enough, considering the circumstances.

I don't know what our altitude was, but as we flew north, in a couple hours, I could see out the window that we were no longer in bright and sunny conditions, but were now flying in clouds and mild turbulence. One of our fellow passengers was a pilot who was making visits up to the cockpit and was letting us know what was happening. He soon told us that there was a massive winter storm lying across the country's midsection and that we might have to forget about flying into Detroit and fly to an alternate airport to the East. When I heard this, my heart sank within me for I could see my chances of getting home in time for Bill's funeral were now falling, just as the outside temperature was dropping in snow and ice.

The reports from the cockpit were getting worse. We were now heading for, of all places, New York City and LaGuardia Field. Oh, NO! We are going the wrong way! We are getting farther and farther from Chicago with every turn of the props.

In a few hours, we were over LaGuardia but we could not land because the field was closed by zero-zero storm conditions. We headed north for Bradley Field in Hartford, Connecticut. I thank God that our pilot in command was an Air Force Major who had a lot of experience for he needed every bit of it to get that C-46 down safely.

His first two attempts were missed approaches during which we almost crashed in the stormy conditions. At one point, I looked out the window as he maneuvered that big airplane like a fighter and I read the word "LAUNDRY" off a smokestack that we narrowly missed! I thought sure that I was a goner! But on the third attempt, he set that aircraft down safely and we stepped out into a foot of snow!

All of us on that airplane thought we were going to Detroit, and now, here we were a thousand or so miles east in Hartford, Connecticut! But at least we were alive and in one piece, thanks to some great flying by our pilot, the Major, name unknown!

Someone rounded up an Army truck, which took us to the railroad station in town. Despite the storm, the trains were still running. My mind was so benumbed with grief that I really don't know what happened to my Army companions except that we all headed south to New York City and then from there who knows where?

I soon found myself aboard a very crowded Pennsylvania Railroad train headed west for Pittsburgh and then Chicago. This trip would take at least twenty hours—maybe much longer if the storm delayed us. The telegram had said that the funeral would be Tuesday morning, and here it was already Monday afternoon.

The hours crept by as the train rolled slowly westward. I was in agony thinking about my beloved dead brother and how my dear mother and Irene and Evie were bearing their wretched grief alone and wondering what had happened to me. What a dismal trip!! I spent the last eight hours, standing on a cold and drafty platform between the passenger cars all the way from Pittsburgh to Union Station in Chicago. I hopped a Van Buren street car west to Wolcott and ran up the stairs to our cottage sobbing like a little boy looking for his mommy! But alas, no mommy to comfort me! It was about 7 P.M. and no one was home! I thought that I had missed the funeral and that they all would be at home waiting for news of me. But no—only a young neighbor girl was there taking care of the house while the whole family was at Hursen's Funeral Chapel where Bill was still being waked! The funeral was not until Wednesday morning! Thank God!! I made it home in time!

I dried my tears and hurried through this cold winter's night over to Hursen's on West Madison Street where, just a few short years ago, I said "Goodbye" to my Dad and then to Uncle Walter.

Billy was there all right, looking so peaceful and serene in the coffin as if taking a little nap. My poor mother and Irene and Evie were inconsolable. We all hugged in a shower of tears. They were glad to see me and, later, when I had told them about my nightmarish trip home, they were relieved that I got there in one piece.

Aunt Irene and Bob's wife, Millie, were there to give whatever help they could in this sad situation. No one could tell me what caused Bill's death except that he died at home in his bed Saturday night, probably from a brain tumor. He had been up and about that Saturday, pacing the floor with a severe headache. Again, no one realized how bad his condition was, including, I suppose, Bill himself. Much later, I found out from one of his teammates that Bill had suffered a head injury in a football game some months before.

The next day we had the funeral Mass at St. Jarlath's and Father O'Brien gave a very touching and moving homily for he had known all our family for many years. Our tears flowed freely.

We buried Bill in the family plot at Mt. Carmel.

Meanwhile, Lois had trouble in Florida trying to get a train reservation to Chicago. It took several days for her to line up a seat on a train headed for home so she missed the sad events on the West Side. Her mother and father, Louise and Fred Bross, met her at Union Station and took her home to Roseland, where I joined her.

Leaving my family in such a pitiful state made me feel awful, but what could I do? I had to get back to my duties at Boca Raton. At least, I had gotten home for the funeral; Bob and Walter both told me later that when they received news of Bill's death, they were shocked and grieved because they were so far from home and unable to console Ma and the rest of us. They loved Bill just as we did but they had to shed their tears alone and far away.

My emergency furlough would soon expire, so Lois and I went by a slow and dirty train ride back down to Florida.

Once there, I immediately applied for Officer's Candidate

School—Engineers, first choice and Infantry, second choice. Lois and I hardly had time to get back into the routine of things when I was notified that I was accepted in Engineers OCS and would ship out in a few days for Fort Belvoir, Virginia. Of course, Lois had to go home. I was thrilled with the splendid opportunity to attend Officer's Candidate School, but I was saddened by our farewell as my dear little wife left for home. I would miss her so much! I hated "goodbyes."

Now, on to Virginia and Engineer's OCS!

Chapter Six
Engineers Officer's Candidate School

It was an even dozen of us who headed north to Fort Belvoir. For the most part, we were in a jolly mood as we faced a new and unknown challenge in our military careers. We were all confident, that in a few months' time, we would be wearing those shiny golden bars on our uniforms; little did we suspect what formidable tasks lay ahead that would bring most of us disappointment and failure.

We were assigned to 2nd Platoon, Company C in the Officer's Candidate Battalion, Corps of Engineers. Of the thirty-five candidates in our platoon, most of them had received their earlier training in the infantry or engineers. When they learned that, here in their midst, was a group of sun-tanned fly-boys from the Air Force in Boca Raton, they laughed themselves silly. We took their razing good-naturedly and hoped to show them that they were wrong in their assessment of our capabilities.

Each platoon had its own Tactical Officer—Tac for short—who would be in charge of our training. Our man was Lieutenant Brower; Lieutenant Rocco had the first platoon and Lieutenant Schmidt led the third platoon. We would meet them shortly.

Our first duty was to officially report to Captain Childs in the company orderly room. We stood in line and nervously waited our turn.

Once inside, the semi-darkened room revealed the Captain sitting behind his desk and in the background, I could see several other human forms. I gave him my best salute—"Sir, Candidate Magrady reporting as ordered."

The Captain returned my salute and began to ask me questions that tested my confidence:

"Do you think that you can field-strip a Garand rifle in front of a platoon?"

"Yes, Sir," I smartly responded.

Voice from the back of the room: "You look like a little boy!"

I made no response to that one.

Captain: "Do you think you can demonstrate how to field-strip a 30-caliber machine gun?"

Me: "Yes, Sir!" (I hoped that I responded with assurance

even though I had never seen a Garand rifle or a 30-caliber machine gun in my whole life!)

Another voice from the back of the room: "Mister, do you play the drums?"

Me: "No, Sir!"

Captain: "What do you know about cover and concealment?"

Me: "Nothing, Sir, but I'll learn all I can!"

Another voice from the back of the room: "Mister, do you play the piano?"

Me: No, Sir."

Same voice: "Get a haircut!"

The Captain dismissed me and I left the orderly room.

Next, we went to the supply room where we were issued a footlocker, a rolled-up mattress, a Garand rifle, and assorted other supplies. We had to carry this heavy load across the company area to our barracks and, of course, you never walked in the company area, but always double-timed.

It was really funny watching each lad trying to double-time carrying that heavy and awkward load! Footlockers and mattresses and rifles were flying all over the place! Once inside our barracks, it was a real chore to carry all that stuff up to the second floor where we bunked. It was not a good beginning!

It was very difficult for us to adapt to a new and rigorous schedule. From 6 o'clock in the morning until 10 o'clock at night every minute was filled with military and technical instruction. After supper, from 7 P.M. until 9 P.M. each evening we sat in Study Hall, where we did our "homework" from assignments that had been handed out during the day. It was here that I became friends with Walter Jordan, the only Black lad in all of C Company.

Walter was from Virginia. His education in grade school and high school was earned at a great cost: he lived several miles from school and there was no bus service, so he had to walk there everyday! We both had much to thank our parents for! I helped Walter with his schoolwork and we leaned on each other to weather the tremendous stress of meeting new challenges everyday.

Also, in our platoon was a large contingent of lads from the University of Michigan. They were upper classmen in engineering who found themselves here at Engineers OCS even though most of them really didn't want this assignment. In a few weeks, most of them walked out. One such fellow was a jovial and happy soldier named Busch, who gave us all a good laugh. It was about the third week in our training when Candidate Busch was assigned the roll of Company Commander (the Captain). Three other Candidates were each in charge of our platoons (Lieutenants). Busch's job was to march the Company out to our first work site of the day; to do this he had to call out verbal orders to keep us on our proper route.

At first, everything went well. We covered the first few

blocks in smart order. Then, Busch's commands became more and more confusing. He had 1st Platoon going one way and 3rd Platoon marching off in the opposite direction and we in the 2nd Platoon were stuck in the middle! The poor "lieutenants" didn't know what to do! Finally, the three Tac Officers who had been marching along beside us took over. They got our three platoons back in proper formation and then; they descended upon poor Mister Busch.

Even though we were standing at attention, I was close enough to see and hear what transpired. The three Tac Officers surrounded Busch, who was standing in the street at strict attention.

"Mister Busch," screamed Lt. Rocco, in Busch's face, "What are you trying to do?"

Busch: No answer.

"Are you crazy?" yelled Lt. Schmidt in Busch's ears. Lt. Brower got into the act with a few loud verbal insults.

I watched Busch's face as he began to wither under this relentless attack. The corners of his mouth started to turn up, and little by little, a big smile crossed his kisser, and then he couldn't help himself any longer—he burst out laughing and the louder the Tacs yelled at him, the more he laughed. Later, we laughed when we could. Sorry to say, Busch was relieved of his command on the spot and, shortly thereafter, washed out of Engineers OCS.

Despite all odds, Walter Jordan and I kept plugging along.

We passed the fifth-week evaluation check and then the ninth-week check. By that time, more than half of Company C and half of our 2nd Platoon had been washed out. What we didn't know at the beginning of our assignment was that this Company C and its three Tac Officers had earned the reputation of being the toughest company in the whole battalion, with the highest percentage of washouts! Now they tell us!!

Combat Engineers do many things. We were expected to be as good as the Infantry in soldiering, but also, be able to build the roads and bridges and layout airfields, and if necessary, blow up the enemy's installations.

Our days were long and hard, both mentally and physically. One night, just after lights out, we were "unwinding" in our upstairs barracks. We had worked very hard in the field all day building a timber trestle bridge and then had double-timed the two miles all the way back to our company area. We were bushed!! But some of the boys were laughing about something that had happened during the day. Our sneaky Tac Officers crept into the barracks and heard the laughter. They snapped on the lights and yelled, "Fall out, five minutes—full-field packs!!"

We couldn't believe our ears, but rushed to get ready. Do you know what they made us do? A five-mile hike in the dark! We didn't get back to our bunks until after midnight, utterly exhausted! After that, we tried to control our "unwinding" a little better, but it was not easy.

Whenever we fell out into a formation in the Company street, we all hurried as fast as we could to avoid being last one out of the barracks and so to avoid the verbal onslaught of the hovering Tac Officers.

On this occasion, I took my place and was standing at attention, but could see what transpired out of the corner of my eye. Practically all the troops were in formation when we heard a loud, rumbling noise as Mister Appeldorf, a tall gangly kid from the 3rd Platoon, came barreling down the stairs and out the door onto the low wooden porch; that's as far as he made it on his feet for he tripped on the porch and flew out into the air, flopping his arms and kicking his legs as he crashed head first into the dirt below.

He didn't move, and we could not move either; I feared for the poor boy's well being. Lt. Schmidt, who had been standing nearby, strode over to the fallen soldier and without showing any concern for his health, blurted out, "Appeldorf, YOU LOOKED JUST LIKE A BIG BIRD!!"

Luckily, the lad was not injured, but soon after, washed out of OCS.

With a lot of hard work and perseverance, Walter Jordan and I made it to the 14th week evaluation when we were told that we needed more time to develop our leadership qualities and that we could either drop out or be washed back to the 9th week of training. We learned that of those men who washed back, practically all of them were eventually commissioned. So we chose to repeat those extra weeks of drudgery and welcomed our transfer out of C Company to Company D.

What a wonderful change! Company D and our new Tac Officer, Lt. Triezenberg made our lives so much easier. The harassing was gone; as long as we completed our tasks with military correctness, our grades were acceptable. The last nine weeks of training just flew by. Walter Jordan and I were commissioned Second Lieutenants in the Corps of Engineers on September 22, 1945.

Of these original 115 candidates in Company C, only 35 were commissioned, of the 12 of us, who came up from Florida, only myself and two others made the grade. Thank You, Lord!!

Lois came out to Fort Belvoir for my graduation ceremony and then we headed for home to enjoy a seven-day leave. My first assignment as a 2nd Lieutenant was as a training officer at Fort Leonard Wood, Missouri.

Here at Fort Leonard Wood, which lies in the rolling hills about 50 miles southwest of St. Louis, I was placed in charge of a platoon of soldiers in Basic Training. A lot of different military activities were ongoing at Fort Leonard Wood, which was an old permanent Army Base, but foremost of which was as a Basic Training Center in the Corps of Engineers.

I thoroughly enjoyed my work as platoon leader. The Army had laid out a nicely designed curriculum—complete with lesson plans and all. Within a few weeks, I confirmed what I had suspected all along—that I loved to teach and that I was good at it! I got along well with my non-coms and with the troops and with the other platoon leaders; the only one who seemed to dislike me and one who had little patience with my inexperience was our Company Commander—a First Lieutenant who hailed from the Deep South. I respected his uniform—but not him!

The weeks passed quickly. Lois came down from Chicago and we found a tiny apartment in nearby Rolla, Missouri. Having her with me made all the difference in the world. But not for long, orders came through for me to report back at Fort Belvoir, Virginia to attend an eight-week class in Engineers Construction School. So Lois went home and I headed east.

By the time I arrived at the Construction School, it had already been in session for a few days and I missed out on much of the work with levels and transits and layouts in general. The training sessions that followed were interesting and varied — hands-on involvement in plumbing, electrical, and carpentry projects, but the best was yet to come.

The landing strip at Fort Belvoir was only about 2,000 feet long, so our class was given the job to plan and layout a thousand-foot extension to the runway. Just being at an airport, even a small one like this, had me walking on clouds!

One morning, Lt. Davis and I were watching four of the Stinson L-19s warm up on the field. He said "Let's go over and see if the pilots will take us up for a ride." Of course, I was in favor of this marvelous suggestion.

We walked over to the airplanes and shook hands with the pilots. They agreed to take us up but warned us that the impending air work was going to include all sorts of combat maneuvers, which could be very rough on queasy passengers. "That's fine with us!" Davis and I replied, as we trotted over to the parachute shanty to pick up our chutes.

The Stinson L-19 is a two-seater—pilot in front. My parachute was a seat type and quite heavy. I put it on and then I was trying clumsily to climb into the back seat of the airplane when my pilot, a "flying Sergeant" laughingly told me to put the chute into the cockpit and then sit on it and hook it up! Much easier when you do it the right way. But later when we were flying, I thought to myself that this chute is so heavy that if I need to bail out, I'd never be able to leave the airplane!

All four L-19s took off, climbed out, and then joined up in echelon formation, further reaching for altitude. The view was magnificent! My heart was pounding as I looked over and waved to Lt. Davis in the next airplane. He was so close I could see by his grinning face that he was enjoying this ride as much as I was.

Up, up, and up we soared! At last, we leveled off and circled, as if to let the powerful Lycoming engines catch their breath! Then the first and lowest airplane in the echelon formation peeled off and dove straight down in a screaming dive toward Mother Earth! Then the second airplane peeled off and followed the first airplane down, down, out of my sight. As I watched, we were third in line so I knew what was soon to follow.

In eager anticipation, I grabbed a hold of the cockpit struts—one in each hand, and then over we went in a violent wingover, move down, streaking toward the ground. My pilot pulled up, with plenty of room to spare, and then hung the L-19 on it prop until I thought sure we would surely stall; but no, that Lycoming 240-hp engine just lifted that sweet little airplane skyward with no sound of complaint.

At altitude again, all four pilots were throwing their airplanes all over the sky—loops, snap rolls, chandelles, Cuban Eights, Immelmanns—the works! After a few of these maneuvers, I felt that I wasn't going to die and that I could let go of the struts. Then, as quickly as the fun started, it was time to return to the same and the predictable. One last thrill—before landing, my pilot flew down the runway, about 20 feet off the ground, then rocked our wings so that the tips came real close to the surface of the runway! A Buzz-job to remember!! What a great ride!!

This building project at the airfield concluded our work at Construction School and we all headed back to our regular assignments. Lois came back to be with me at Fort Leonard Wood, but not for long. In a few weeks, orders came through for me to report to a training battalion at Fort Lewis, Washington. By this time in February 1946, the war had ended, so Lois accompanied me on the long train ride westward.

On the way, I picked up a short-term flu bug and spent a day in a hotel in Portland, Oregon—sicker than a dog!

Eventually, I reported to my new Company Commander at Fort Lewis. This was a training battalion similar to the one at Fort Leonard Wood, with one exception: our trainees were all black! Captain Roberts and his other two platoon leaders, Lt. Short and Lt. Shureck, returned from combat in Europe and were now marking time training troops until their separation came through.

These men were really great to work with. Lt. Short had received a battlefield commission and was now a modest platoon leader in a training company; Lt. Shureck had dodged his share of German bullets to lead troops across the Rhine River and was now trying desperately to get every pretty girl in the Northwest into his tiny coupe—"Shureck's Shack Trap!"

Lois and I found a nice second floor apartment in a white frame house in Tacoma, Washington—only a few miles from camp. Lois' father had taught her how to drive when she was in high school. Used cars, then, were hard to find, but she bought a 1933 second-hand Chevrolet sedan for $350 and started the daunting task of teaching me to drive it. After a few harrowing episodes behind the wheel, I had the nerve to drive our buggy back and forth to camp. The Good Lord must have been watching over me for I had no accidents—just blowouts from those worn tires. One time a rear tire blew so hard that the hubcap flew off over an embankment and is probably still rolling!

Springtime comes early in the Northwest and in a few months, I learned that I was going to be separated from service during the first week of July. Great News!! Even though our stay here was filled with happy times, and Lois had taken a job on the base, we both were looking forward to going home to Chicago—to stay put for a while.

In June, Lois' father and mother, Fred and Louise Bross, drove all the way out to Tacoma from Chicago in their 1941 Ford Coupe. We had plenty of room in our apartment, so they stayed with us until my separation came through. Meanwhile, we showed them the sights in the beautiful Northwest.

One such memorable visit was up to Paradise Valley on Mount Rainier. It was sunny and warm when we left Tacoma, but by the time we had ascended the five thousand feet or so up to Paradise Valley, there was still ten feet of snow on the ground and many of the skiers were in shorts! The weather was a little murky and clouds covered the top of the mountain, but still, to look up at that awesome sight was an experience of a lifetime!

On July 11, 1946, my separation from the U.S. Army at Fort Lewis was quick and painless. We had packed up everything at the house in Tacoma and were ready to begin our long, but happy trip *home*!

Chapter Seven
Home, Sweet Home

Fred Bross was an excellent driver who loved to put his cars through their paces over the road—the longer the road, the better. I guess that is why he and Louise decided to drive all the way out to Tacoma from Chicago when my separation from service became imminent. He kept his 1941 Ford Coupe in top condition and covered the long trip out without mishap. It took five days to complete the two-thousand-plus mile journey, usually starting out early in the morning and then getting off the road by two or three in the afternoon. Motels were few and far between then and, besides, it was July, a peak travel time.

So Lois and I (luckily, two small people) took our places in the small rear seats of Fred's 1941 Ford Coupe and happily let him do all the driving. Louise could drive very capably and so could Lois, but I was just a beginner. Fred took the wheel, and never let go! We were comfortable in the back and enjoyed the marvelous scenery as we traversed the Rockies and rolled into the high plains—each day bringing us closer to home. As we neared Chicago, my heart began to beat faster as it always did on my returning—Chicago, my town! Chicago, my home! The big lump in my throat must have been a lump of love!

But this time it was a lot different. While we were away, Lois' folks had set up a small apartment for us in their building on 114th Place in Roseland, the far south side of town. What a marvelous gift for our homecoming! And this was just the first of the many occasions when Fred and Louise gave us a supporting hand when we needed it.

The Bross homestead was a large two-story house that originally had been two nine-room apartments. I'm sure Fred and Louise had their three daughters in mind when they surveyed the possibilities of their recent purchase. With great energy and imagination, matched well by their talent with tools and construction equipment, they converted the two nine-room apartments into a four flat—almost completely unaided.

Fred worked full time as a machinist, so Louise did most of the work, as well as any man could do, in transforming their house. Each front apartment had five rooms—kitchen, dining room, front parlor and two bedrooms, while the smaller rear apartments had kitchen, living room, bedroom and an enclosed rear porch that served as a three-season additional room.

We lived downstairs, in the back apartment while Lois' older sister Florence (Tootie) and her husband, Johnny, lived in the front, along with Johnny's little daughter, Carolyn. Fred and Louise lived upstairs in the front apartment with Lois' younger sister, Ethel (Tuppie). Upstairs, the back apartment was rented to Ronnie and Helen Wieck and their two young children, Carol and Eddie. A cement side-drive led all the way back to the two-car garage.

In July 1946, there was in vogue what was known to returning servicemen as the "52-20 Club." The U.S. government would pay us $10 per week, for up to 52 weeks, while we looked for jobs. While many of the veterans took advantage of this dole and took their time in finding employment, I was not one of them. In less than two weeks, I found a job out at U.S. Steel, South Works, as a laboratory technician. Here, I learned to run chemical tests on the steel samples as the product was being made. I enjoyed this work very much, but I could not get used to changing shifts every seven days or so.

In six months time, I left the steel mill to go to work in the U.S. Stockyards—Wilson & Co., again as a lab technician in the margarine department. This job was steady days, with weekends off but entailed a long, long streetcar ride (1 hour, 10 minutes). All the while, at the mill or in the stockyard, I dreamed about going back to college to try to get a degree in education so that I could become a teacher.

Lois and I talked it over and with the help of the G.I. Bill I enrolled at DePaul University in September 1947. The first semester I was in Liberal Arts College on the north side, but on the advice of my brother Bob, in the second semester I switched over to the Business School downtown. My class work was in the morning so I was able to work part-time afternoons at Boreva Sportswear in the Loop. Even though, my grades at DePaul were good, at the end of the 1948 school year, I decided to go back to work, this time I'd try my luck at sales.

To be an outside salesperson, you need a car; so we bought a 1938 4-cylinder Willys Coupe for $385.00. That little blue coupe was in sad shape, but somehow, with the help of my local auto mechanic, Bill Ores, it kept running—patched up, wired up, four on the floor, even with skid chains during the winter!

Meanwhile, in the summer of 1947, Fred and Louise had bought a lot on Big Lake Chetac in northern Wisconsin and had started work on a summerhouse. Lois and I needed a vacation, so I asked my ole pal, Joe Germanos, to come along to help with the driving. Joe had made it home from service in good shape and was still single. He loved fishing so he jumped at the chance to go with us. During the war, Joe had a lot of experience learning to drive all sorts of vehicles at the Aberdeen Proving Grounds in Maryland.

When we pulled up in front of his house in the Willys, Joe just rolled his eyes while his mother covered hers! "Four hundred and twenty miles in that crate?" he howled. "It'll be okay," I replied.

We were loaded to the gills, and the little four-cylinder

engine huffed and puffed, especially up that big, long hill at Baraboo. Joe drove all night, in the rain, with me talking my head off to keep him awake, while Lois slept peacefully in the backseat. We had to stop several times to put grease in the water pump, but we made it all the way north and this began Joe's and our love affair with Wisconsin's North Woods!

This part of the North Woods was not entirely new to the Brosses. Louise's brothers, Jack and Matt Tills, both owned small resorts here on Lake Chetac and it was from Jack that Louise bought their gorgeous half-acre lot on high ground overlooking the lake. Nearby, around the adjacent point was Matt Tills' resort where the Brosses had rented cottages during previous vacations.

Work on the house had only recently begun, so the garage was the only completed section while the rest of the structure had only the foundation. There was room enough for Fred and Louise and Lois and me, but Joe had to go down the road a mile or so to rent a sleeping room in Lewis Lodge. He didn't mind that as long as he could spend plenty of time in the boat fishing.

We didn't own a boat at that time so Jack let us use one of his. Joe already knew how to handle a rowboat, but Lois and I were novice seamen. We had to row around our Badger Bay because we had no outboard motor. That was okay, because it seemed like the fish were all around us and we caught plenty of pan fish and once in awhile, a walleye or a northern.

At night, we fished off the wooden pier. You never knew

what was going to bit your bait next—could be a bluegill or crappie, or a monster northern or a fat walleye! What great fun!!

The few days that we could spend in this wonderland were soon over—our jobs called us back to work, so we packed up for the long trip home. Will the Willys make it?

Again, Joe did most of the driving. I took my turn to give him a break, but I could tell that he was uneasy while I was at the wheel, mostly because of my inexperience. The same steep hills that gave the Willys' little engine fits on the way up were still there on the way back but, somehow, that tiny coupe, with several stops to grease the water pump, made the long trek home (fifteen hours).

I needed a better car for my work in food sales, so we traded in the Willys on a new 1949 Plymouth Coupe. Lois worked at the White Castle at 111th and State for fifteen months to help pay off our car loan ($87 per month). Lois' folks charged us only $25 per month rent for our little apartment, and even then, some months we had trouble getting our $25 together. That car payment was a killer and, in addition, we had a small monthly payment at Hatton Furniture Store for living room furniture. Somehow, we managed.

Lois' family had always loved their pets—both dogs and cats (and even rabbits). So one fine day, Louise gave us a present—a small tan and white puppy, a mixed breed but a loveable little hound! We named her Rusty and at once she became our constant companion, at play in the side drive or for rides in the car. There was always someone at home to walk our dogs in the back alley. That's one advantage of living in a multiple-family situation—there's usually someone nearby to give a helping hand.

They say time passes quickly when you're having fun! These early months and years of our marriage flew by for Lois and for me. My work in food sales did not pay much but I enjoyed what I was doing, even though I could have given a stronger effort. Whenever we had a few days off work, or a brief vacation, we drove up to the Woods to give a hand in the construction of the Bross' summerhouse. On one such visit, I helped the carpenter frame the roof on the fish house.

Louise spent a lot of time up there and even laid the asphalt tiles on the floor throughout the whole house! A splendid job!! She also helped her brother, Jack Tills, install the plumbing in the house and in the garage. What a talented lady! Fred would go up when he could, driving his '49 Lincoln Sedan, pulling a trailer loaded with odds and ends from home.

Meanwhile, Bob Magrady was helping the Magradys on Warren Avenue dispose of some of their properties. They had not been out to Cedar Lake, Indiana, for many years, so he asked me if I wanted to buy the place with him as a partner. I jumped at the chance and we picked it up for a song.

The cottage needed a lot of work, so the first thing we did was to put on a new roof—first, layers of tar paper, then new asphalt shingles. With the help of young Tom Fahey, Bob and

I finished the job in one day. Later on, Bob painted the whole cottage by himself, which took up several days of his summer vacation.

In front of the cottage was a huge hedge that had been growing wild for many years. I tackled that job one beautiful morning and hacked, and sawed, and trimmed all day long, until late in the afternoon, the hedge finally looked like a hedge again.

The grass, too, around the place was about knee-high, but was no match for the new power lawn mower that we bought. Little by little, the cottage was starting to shape up.

Of course, Rusty always accompanied us on our trips to Cedar Lake and she loved to chase the varmints in the high grass behind the cottage. This one afternoon while Lois and I were busy doing something or other, we lost track of her; when we noticed that Rusty was nowhere to be seen, we began calling her and whistling for her to come back. Just about that time, when "Panic" was about to set in, here she came trudging slowly out of the swamp behind the house. She was a sight! She was covered with mud and slime from head to toe and no matter how hard she shook herself, she was still a mess! After a good scolding, we all had to laugh at this wild and crazy dog! Into the tub at the pump, we soaked her to start a much-needed bath.

While we owned the cottage, we did not see Brother Bob that often; nor did we discuss with him what future plans we may have had for the cottage. We just figured that, in time, we would fix the place up to make it livable. That is why when he called me to say that he had sold the cottage and the five lots for $1,500, it was a huge shock! He didn't even talk it over with us at all! Kiss it Goodbye!!

Chapter Eight
Railway Mail Clerk

In the year right after the war, Lois and I made many trips from the South Side to the West Side. Ma and Evie were still living in the house at 325 S. Wolcott, while Irene and her growing family lived next door in the basement at 323 S. Wolcott. Brother Bob had taken over the properties for the Aunts and Uncles on Warren Avenue and now he decided to sell 325 to the Bredemeirs Factory in the back so that trucks coming into their loading dock could have easier access. At the same time, he bought the 323 building from the Magradys. Our dearly beloved, but ramshackle cottage at 325 was quickly demolished and turned into a vacant lot. Ma moved in with Bob and Millie in the middle apartment at 323, while Evie moved in with he new husband, Ray Adams, who had a room over on Jackson Boulevard.

Evie had been seeing Ray for sometime now and they

decided to tie the knot. Lois and I witnessed the simple ceremony down at St. Jarlath's. Ray was a graduate of the famous Boystown in Omaha, Nebraska. He served in the Air Force in the South Pacific during the war and now made Chicago his home.

After a few months, Bob rented the third-floor apartment to Evie and Ray and Ma moved upstairs to live with them because she rarely saw Bob or Millie. They apparently ate their meals at Millie's house on Damen Avenue next to Sawyer & Allen Drugstore. Evie was soon with child and later when Baby Raymond was born, Ma became a live-in babysitter.

Meanwhile, my work in sales came to what appeared to be a dead end. I realized, at last, that I was no salesman and like a lot of returning servicemen, I was searching for that "better job." Both Brother Bob and Uncle Willie had long, successful careers in the United States Post Office. The pay was not that great, nor was the work glamorous, but it was rock-solid steady—even during the Great Depression.

I saw a notice in a newspaper that an exam was coming up for employment as a clerk in the Railroad Transportation Division or Railway Mail Service, as it was called. I took the test and came out with a high score, and along with the additional ten points I got for being a veteran; my total grade assured me of being called to work in the near future.

While waiting to be called by the Post Office, Lois and I took an extended vacation up north at the cottage. Here we stayed with Fred and Rusty for the entire month of June. We were blessed with glorious weather, and the fishing was great. Fred didn't go out with us in the boat, but every evening as we came in with our catch, he was there on the bank to check our basket and to voice his approval. We spent many happy hours in the fish house cleaning our catch. There I learned never to put your thumb in a bullhead's mouth even though you think he is cold-stone dead after whacking him with a rubber mallet. I made the mistake of putting my thumb in this huge bullhead's mouth, as I was getting ready to skin him. Well, he clamped down hard on my thumb and there I was, dancing around the fish house with this horny devil dangling from my hand. Of course, I was yelling and Lois was laughing her head off! Finally, he let go and dropped on the floor. You can bet your sweet life that I smacked him a few more times with the rubber mallet.

We will never forget that month of June on beautiful Lake Chetac.

Eventually, the Post Office called me and I reported to the unit at Midway Airport—55th and Cicero Avenue. Here I joined a group of young men who hailed from all over the Midwest—but mostly from Illinois and Indiana. We were all trainees now with the challenge of learning how to be good mail clerks. Most of us thought that we would go to work right away in the mail cars on the trains, but that would come later, after several months training at Midway.

Our bosses, although very strict, were good teachers. They

didn't tolerate any goofing around. To begin, they showed us how to work a first-class letter case, then how to study a scheme. At that time, in the early fifties, every railway mail clerk had to learn a new scheme—usually 1,200 post offices in a state, every six months. That meant that you were always studying—if you wanted to keep your job.

They started us out with the 1,200 post offices of northern Illinois. I had a cardboard letter case at home to practice on. Getting ready for that first test was really scary because we didn't know what to expect. Turns out they gave us a hundred post offices to throw; you had to get a score of at least 95% correct, or you flunked the test. My studying at home paid off and I passed with only one mistake. But that is one part of that job that I never liked—you always knew that your next exam was coming due soon and you had better get studying. Before leaving the Postal Service, I learned the schemes for the states of Illinois, Indiana, Iowa, Pennsylvania, and New York.

While we were learning how to be good mail clerks at Midway, we were becoming acquainted with the railway post offices and the railroads that carried them. You didn't have to go on the road if you didn't want to but you could stay at Midway or apply for transfer elsewhere. I applied for the Chicago and Omaha Post Office that ran on Northwestern trains between Chicago and Omaha, Nebraska.

The mail cars on these trains were actually complete mobile post offices manned by a crew of five or six clerks, depending on its size. The clerk-in-charge usually worked the lead letter case; two or three clerks worked other letter cases, or newspaper and magazine tables; the clerk in the rear of the car had the toughest job—handling the parcel post and making pickups and dispatches on the fly.

My first assignment on the road was as a substitute for the parcel post clerk in the rear of the mail car on the Chicago and Omaha Post Office. Another member of the crew handled the hard job while I worked a letter case. The white-haired clerk-in-charge knew that a greenhorn like me could never do a passable job in the back of the car. Whenever a regular crewmember missed a trip and they sent out a substitute, it meant that the rest of the crew had to pitch in and do extra work to make up for the lack of experience in the sub.

This kindly, old clerk-in-charge took me under his wing and started to "show me the ropes." I had reported to him at the Northwestern Station at 9:00 P.M. and the train began to roll about 11:00 P.M. We had time to take our mail on board, set up our letter cases and parcel post racks.

This was a fast train that made only a few stops along the way so that meant the "hook" would make pickups as the leather mail pouches were thrown out the side door.

Along the side of the mail car was a long metal arm that was attached to a wooden handle inside the car. When the clerk pushed down on this handle, the "hook" would extend out a few feet from the side of the car. At small towns, where the train passed through at full speed, a small leather mail pouch was hung up on framework close to the tracks so that if the "hook" was extended, it would make the pickup. At the same time, the clerk threw a small mail pouch out of the door, supposedly to a known target.

Sometimes, with the train moving at 80 miles an hour, in the darkness of the night, in the zero cold of winter, with the clerk hanging out the open door with his eyes straining to see through his goggles, it has been known that instead of hitting his target, the errant flying mail pouch flew through the windows of the station waiting room or else knocked a startled guest out of the nearby outhouse!

Of course, he had to make the pickup at the precise moment that he was making the toss!

I worked that letter case all night long, with timeout for lunch, gradually getting used to the smooth rhythmic rolling of the mail car on the rails. We pulled into Omaha station about 7 o'clock in the morning, unloaded our mail and greeted the next crew who would take this train the rest of the way to Denver, Colorado.

Most of the mail clerks stayed at the Rome Hotel in Omaha for their layover for $2 a night. But my boss took me with him to a place where he said was just as good as the Rome but only charged 50 cents per night. It was my first and last time to stay at such a place because it was not much better than an ordinary flophouse! After that, on subsequent visits, the Rome Hotel, with very nice comfortable accommodations, became my resting place in Omaha.

We reported back to work at 1:00 P.M. the next day as our crew took over the mail car on the incoming train. Once again, I worked a letter case for the eight-hour run into Chicago. By the time I got home, I was really tired but well pleased with this new and exciting experience of working on the road. I had several days off to rest up and to look forward to my next assignment.

Most of the regulars working the mail cars were the best in their profession. I would call them the "elite" of the postal system. They took great pride in their work and how they handled each and every piece of mail. When they looked at an address on a letter or package, they knew the very best way to get that piece "home" because they were up on their schemes and because they kept their routing books up to date with the latest changes. Many of these clerks were farmers or guys who lived in small towns out in Illinois, or Iowa, or Indiana, who commuted into Chicago or Omaha to begin their runs. They were the best!

I worked on the road over a year and made many runs on the fast trains to Omaha and more runs on the slow trains out to Boone, Iowa. I even had the marvelous experience of riding on the fireman's open-window side of a giant steam locomotive. The slow trains were more fun! But all the while, in the back of my mind, I still dreamed about being a teacher. I had accumulated about two years of college credits and to get my degree, I would need at least two more years of college courses. I could not go to school while working on the road, so I decided to accept a regular assignment at the postal unit at Midway Airport. It was not as exciting as working on a mail train but here I could make plans to continue my education.

In the summer of 1954, I applied and, after a battery of tests, was accepted as a regular student at the University of Chicago, Hyde Park Campus. They scrutinized my academic work at Yale and at DePaul and placed me at the Junior Level in the English Department.

My job at Midway was working the airmail parcel post rack on the 4–12 afternoon shift. It was not physically draining, so I thought I could go to school full time and continue to work full time. Big Mistake!! Throughout the fall and winter of 1954-55, I did my best to keep up with the course work at school, but it was more than I could handle, and for the first time in my academic career, I actually received an "F" in my Shakespeare course. I was shocked and mortified! A buddy of mine at work, Glen Sprouse, after watching me struggle to keep my academic ship afloat without success, gave me the following advice: quit this job and concentrate on your educational goals—work somewhere part time if necessary. Good advice!!

I left the employment of the U.S. Postal Department in the summer of 1955. I gave up those steady bi-monthly checks with much fear and trepidation. Lois was working and we lived very frugally in our small apartment—we were not in debt (before the days of plastic charge cards) because we only bought what we could pay for. My immediate plan was to work for the degree full time and to find some kind of part-time job to help pay our bills.

After that humiliating experience of actually receiving a failing grade at the University of Chicago, I admitted to myself that super-charged academic environment was more than I could handle. The English Department at Chicago left a bad taste in my mouth, so I decided to change schools and to change my major to history at Roosevelt University where I enrolled for the fall semester.

During that summer of 1955, I gave driving lessons for Safeway Driving School, which was affiliated with the YMCA. The students would attend classroom sessions for eight hours, and then they would come to us for eight hours of roadwork, ending happily with their driver's license. But some applicants were not capable of driving a vehicle safely and were denied the license.

A few of these students were ones who already had attended other driving school programs and had failed the state tests. They came to Safeway hoping that we could work miracles. We tried our best—but, in some cases, our best was not good enough.

One such lady was a middle-aged professor with a PhD from the University of Chicago who had purchased a new car and then set out to learn to drive it. She was a terrible driver!! She had already flunked out of another driving school when she came to me. She said, "I don't see why I can't drive this car! I have a PhD!" I worked with her for eight hours and then when she demanded that I take her to the state examiner's office, I gave in and reluctantly set up the test. She failed miserably! When the examiner brought her back from the test, I thought he was going to hit me! "You had a lot of nerve to bring that woman here," he growled. "She almost killed me!"

Another problem student was a very nice intelligent middle-aged man, probably in his forties. He had been to other driving schools and never passed. And I could see why. This guy was like "Jekyll and Hyde." Before he got behind the wheel, he seemed pleasant and relaxed, but as soon as he took hold of the steering wheel, everything changed. His body stiffened up, he clenched his teeth mightily, and his fingers tightened around the wheel in a death grip. And when he moved the shifting gear, he almost tore it off the steering column. I tried to get him to relax, but to no avail. One day, in a heavily peopled shopping area, he almost drove into a group of folks in a crosswalk. After that, I sadly told him to forget about driving, once and for all, before he killed someone. I don't know if he took my advice or not.

One of my pupils was a very large, but very sweet older black lady. She would come for her lesson and I would drive the car to the practice area. She would get behind the wheel and then she just wanted to talk. We would talk about driving and about cars, and talk about her family, and talk about my family, and talk about everything else! And, do you know, in several hours of lessons, we never left the curb!

Teaching driving was a marvelous experience. I met a lot of wonderful people and I learned a lot about them and a lot about myself.

Chapter Nine
So Long, Post Office—
Hello, Roosevelt University

What about the Aunts and Uncles over on Warren Avenue? After the War, all of our lives were profoundly and drastically changed. With school and jobs to attend to, Lois and I had our hands full and had difficulty even finding time to visit Ma and the girls and it seemed like the only time we saw the Aunts and Uncles was when one of them was sick enough to be in the hospital—and then the outcome was usually fatal.

Aunt Irene's husband, Uncle Roy, was the first to die in the winter of 1949. That left Aunt Irene alone in that large, old frame house several doors east of the brownstone residence where Uncle Bill, Aunt Eva, and Aunt Anna lived. Uncle George had his own house over on Washington Boulevard—

complete with a younger live-in! She was supposed to be a deep, dark family secret, but everyone knew about her.

Aunt Irene managed to hang on until the winter of 1954, when she needed Hursen's funeral services over on Madison Street. With all the business that the Magrady family gave the Hursen's over the years, beginning with Ethel's death in 1912, you would think that a discount might be forthcoming, but NO!

Later that same year, Aunt Eva suffered a terrible stroke while attending a service downtown at St. Peter's with Aunt Anna. She died a few days later and, once, again, Hursen's was our familiar but sorrowful place to exchange hugs and tears.

Uncle Bill and Aunt Anna were left in the big house. The following summer, June 1955, Lois and I went to see Uncle Bill in St. Anne's Hospital. He had cancer of the larynx and was knocking on death's door. He said, "I'm not afraid to die because I did not live a sinful life." We admired his courage and his faith in God. He died soon after our visit. Back to St. Malachy's and Hursen's.

The Magradys on Warren Avenue always talked about moving "West." For many years, as we were growing up, before the War, that was one of their favorite topics of how they were going to sell all their west-side properties and move to Oak Park! It is sad to say that they never made it! The only one to ever live in Oak Park was Aunt Anna who later lived in one of Brother Bob's buildings near the Oak Park Hospital.

It was Bob Magrady who shouldered the load when the older

Magradys became old and sickly and barely able to take care of themselves, let alone taking care of rental properties. Evie and Irene and Walter were all busy raising their own families and I was involved with getting an education while working part time. Somehow Bob found the time and the energy to help the Magradys in all their needs. Walter and Mary had bought a stucco house in Oak Park some time earlier; Irene and Lee moved their family to a house on Johnson Avenue in Hammond, Indiana.

It was a time when neighborhoods were changing color, almost overnight! Blacks were moving into the West Side in great numbers and the phenomenon that came to be known as "white flight" made its appearance as whites headed for Oak Park and points "west." Even businesses along West Madison Street were closing shop and looking elsewhere for customers. Hursen's Funeral Home on Madison was one of these old establishments to go to the suburbs, so when Uncle George "bit the dust" in 1958, Bob took charge of the arrangements.

Poor Uncle George! He had no insurance so Bob, thinking that he would have to pay for everything, sought out the lowest price funeral that the new undertakers in the Hursen Bldg. could provide, and, let one tell you, that what followed was an economy funeral to remember! No wake, just a short service on Saturday morning. No pallbearers, just the funeral director and two helpers to carry Uncle George out in a cheap wooden coffin. All of us kids were there and we noticed that the funeral director was wearing two different shoes—one wingtip and the other plain toe; and one of his helpers wore no socks!

We laughed about that for years to come! Brother Walter, always the jokester, said that for a few more dollars, the director would wear matching shoes and his helper would wear socks!

Uncle George didn't seem to mind, as he joined his family at Mt. Carmel.

~~~~~~~~~~~

When not busy burying Aunts and Uncles, we all had our own lives to live, our own goals to pursue—our own dreams to dream.

My decision to attend Roosevelt University full time turned out to be one of the wisest I had ever made. The course work in the History Department and the education courses I needed to become a teacher were interesting and manageable. The next two years were a happy time for me because I was able to hold a B+ average in my grades, which qualified me for a limited "B" scholarship that gave me a fifteen percent reduction in my tuition. My G.I. Bill had run out so I was paying my own way then.

In the fall of 1955, Charlie La Roche, Lois' sister's, Ethel's, husband, lined me up for a job working for the Fruit Growers'

Express Company in the Riverdale-Dolton railroad yard. It didn't pay much but the staggered work schedule that included weekends was such that I could maintain a full program downtown; also I found plenty of time between chores, when I could do my schoolwork in the yard office. This job was only for the winter months, but it was perfect for my situation and I worked there again the following winter.

There were many times, while working toward graduation and the degree, when I doubted that I would make it. I had to peel back the layers of my life to see who I really was. I'm sure that God, and my wife, and my family helped me along in so many ways. A very wise teacher once told us that getting an education is 2% inspiration, but 98% perspiration.

One of my last courses before graduation was Practice Teaching at Farragut High School in Chicago. Mr. Miller, my Master Teacher there, gave me full reign in his two classes of juniors in American History. It was a marvelous experience and I did a good job with his help and guidance. The only problem I had there was with my supervising professor from Roosevelt—a Mrs. Henry. For some reason or other, after she sat in several of my classes, she gave me a "D" for my first grade in the course. I think she did so because I didn't always agree with her critiques. I was fighting a losing battle and I didn't know it. Mr. Miller then stepped in and gave me some sound advice. Go along with Mrs. Henry and agree with everything she says; you need her passing grades to graduate, and once you get your degree, you can teach "your way" once again.

I took his advice and spent the rest of the semester "buttering up" Mrs. Henry. She gave me a "B" for my final grade! A lesson well learned!

At long last, after years of toil and trouble, I received my B.A. from Roosevelt University in September 1957. Lois and my two brothers, Bob and Walter, were at my graduation ceremony. It was kind of a special day for us because I was the only one in our family to earn a college degree.

Now, to find a teaching job!

Chapter Ten

A Teacher, at Last!

While practice teaching at Farragut High School, the principal there said that maybe he would have a job for me that fall in the English Department—but it never materialized. I gave up thinking about teaching in Chicago so I turned my searching toward the south suburbs. I heard about an opening in, of all places, Calumet City.

Lincoln School was a K-8 school in a quiet residential neighborhood. Although I was trained to be a high school history teacher, at this time, I was prepared to accept almost any teaching position, even at the grade school level.

Mr. Harris, the superintendent-principal of this self-integrated school district, welcomed me into his office. He was not at all what I expected a principal to look like. It was still warm weather, so that, maybe, is why he had on just a dress shirt, open at the neck, no tie, and his face was covered with a beard of several days growth. In short, he looked like a bum!

He told me about the opening—teaching a sixth grade class—and when he learned all about my training, his remarks seemed to indicate that the job was mine, if I wanted it. So I said, "I'll take the job!" And he replied, "Now, wait a minute— I haven't offered you the job yet!" Wow! What is going on here? Then, he said, "Now, do you want to teach that sixth grade class?" "Yes," I replied. "Okay, the job is yours."

That opening conversation should have tipped me off. I was to spend the next five years working for a man who didn't have all his oars in the water!

Lincoln School, it turns out, was overcrowded. I had to meet my class, for the first time, in a temporary location in the school gymnasium. When the boys and girls began filing in and taking their places, I thought that they looked awfully small for sixth graders. But they were quiet and respectful and listened well to my every word. This first class of mine became one of my all time favorites.

Having well-behaved pupils makes teaching a joy. A long time ago, in one of his TV broadcasts, Bishop Fulton J. Sheen stressed the point that to be an effective parent or teacher, you must temper discipline with love. This I tried to do in my classroom, as well as throw in a joke now and then to relieve the monotony of learning.

Besides being blessed with great kids in my first teaching

assignment at Lincoln School, I was fortunate to meet and become friends with some wonderful teachers. John Masla, shop teacher and basketball coach, and Paul Radjeski, social studies, were extremely helpful in making my initiation pleasant and rewarding. Both of them had been working there for sometime and had good rapport with parents and students.

Another new friend was Carol Prystalski who was a beginning teacher like me. She taught the first grade and lived in the Pullman area of Chicago. Carol had taken the exams to teach in Chicago, but unfortunately, she failed the science portion of the test by only one point, so they disqualified her. As the following years would prove, Chicago had lost the services of a great teacher, while Calumet City reaped the reward. Carol did not drive, so she became my traveling companion to and from school. Because we were pretty much in the same boat, we would talk over the events of the day, our little successes, our many problems, and what worked, and what failed. Carol gave me a discipline tip that she used in her classroom but one that I found difficult to follow in my room that is: "Don't Smile Until Christmas!" Even so, she had a great sense of humor, and we laughed a lot during those five years that I was her chauffer.

That first school year literally flew by! There was more work teaching sixth grade than I realized. In our educational areas, at least, Mr. Harris made sense. He had a rule, that before you left the building on Friday afternoon, you had to turn in your lesson plan book with detailed plans for the following week. This was an excellent idea for it forced us to look at our immediate goals and to think about our plans down the line. If a teacher had to miss school, for whatever reason, the substitute had lesson plans to follow so as to avoid gaps in the teaching process.

But Mr. Harris had some strange ideas, as well. At a teachers' meeting, he said, "Here at Lincoln School, we don't call it "homework"—we refer to it as "work you can do at home!" I saw a few teachers roll their eyes at that one! For the most part, though, he did leave us to be "Lord and Masters" in our own classrooms.

At the end of the school year, most of us renewed our contracts to teach at Lincoln the following year—with the exception of Paul Radjeski, who took a job teaching history over at the local high school, Thornton Fractional North. I envied Paul in his new position because I always wanted to teach history, but I soon learned that, in life, we always don't get "peaches & cream," but sometime something less "yummy!" The Good Lord, in many cases, sends us not what we want, but what we need. In a few short years Paul moved up the line in education from history teacher to principal of Thornton Fractional North High School.

Meanwhile, at Lincoln School, I was blessed with good classes every year. Sure, in almost every group of pupils, you are bound to have one or two kids who seem to have more problems than the rest; but good parents produce good kids and here at Lincoln, these parents, who were mostly hardworking men and women, who respected the power of education, gave us their complete cooperation. At teacher-parent conference times, it was always the same story: the parents of the good kids were there to discuss their children's progress, while the parents (or parent) of the problem child, never showed their faces.

The only boy that I ever failed was one who was the son of a man who owned and ran a notorious nightclub in Calumet City. It was said that this guy belonged to "the Outfit" from Chicago. Well, young "Pete" saw no need to follow instructions or to learn math, for instance, because the "Old Man" would take care of his future. Mr. Harris told me later, that when the "Old Man" learned that I had failed "Pete," he was furious and threatened to come upstairs and "work me over!" Thank God he didn't do that. Who said teaching was dull!

In the fall of 1960, I agreed to teach a fifth grade class. As the first few weeks passed, I was so pleased that these boys and girls were just as nice and eager to learn as were my previous classes. I looked forward to another happy time doing my life's work. But I was wrong. Fate dealt me a low blow!

For the past several years, my mother had been living with Evie and Ray in their apartment in Oak Park. Lois and I made regular Sunday visits over to the West Side to visit Ma and Evie and to attend family get-togethers at holiday times. Ma's health was not particularly poor even though she had a heart problem and diabetes. Sometimes we take our loved ones for granted and we expect them to be with us forever. So when that call came on that Saturday night in October that Ma was in St. Anne's Hospital and we better get right over there, it was a shock!

Bob had taken her to the doctor earlier that day and when the doctor examined her, he said to take her right to the hospital. We arrived at St. Anne's a couple hours after she was admitted and the news was not good. Apparently, Ma was undergoing a massive heart attack and when we came to her room, several nurses and a doctor were with her and they would not let us in. As we passed, the door opened briefly and we could see them trying to get Ma to sit up and Ma looked our way and she had a fearful look on her face. That was the last time we saw her alive. After a few minutes, the doctor came out of her room and said, "Your mother has expired. You were kind of expecting it, weren't you?" No, we weren't! I was flabbergasted, as were Lois and Evie. But Brother Bob, as usual, took the sad news cool as a cucumber. He wanted to talk about Ma's funeral arrangements, but all I wanted to do then was to cry. I loved my mother with all my heart and her sudden unexpected death knocked me for a loop. When my father died when I was fifteen and a junior in high school, it was not nearly this bad, mostly because my dad had been sick for two years and we knew that his end was near. But Ma's sudden demise was a terrible blow. Two afternoons later, I was weeping in the washroom at

Ahern's Funeral Parlor when Brother Bob came in and saw me crying. "What's wrong?" he asked. What's wrong, indeed!!

Ma joined Pa and Bill and the rest of the Magradys out at Mt. Carmel.

In my grief, I turned to God and asked Him to help me get through this difficult time. He did help me for the rest of the school year passed smoothly and quickly, despite my heavy heart.

Better days were coming!

Chapter Eleven
Walking on the Wings
of the Wind

I cannot remember when I did not love airplanes. As a small lad growing up on Chicago's West Side, I watched a beautiful gull-winged monoplane pass over our house regularly as it toured the Loop and then returned to the southwest. When I got older and could make streetcar trips to Chicago Municipal Airport (now Midway), I discovered that this was the home of the beautiful, black and red Stinson Reliant that gave rides for five dollars over downtown Chicago.

Less than perfect vision kept me on the ground in World War II...a bitter disappointment! After the war, I finished college and started a teaching career that gave me enough money to think about taking flying lessons. But career and family considerations postponed my original sortie into aviation until 1961.

From the very beginning, you could say that my flight training was very sporadic. I have always admired the young man or woman who starts out in military or civilian flying and progresses nicely from solo to private pilot to instrument and multi-engine ratings...on up the line in regular, timely increments. No so with me. Better to have done it my way, herky-jerky with long absences from flight, than not at all.

Lansing, Illinois Airport (Chicago-Hammond) in the 60s had crisscrossed grass runways, and it was there that I took my first lessons in Piper J-5As with 90-hp Continental engines. In my first four sessions of an hour each, I was given three different instructors.

Bob initiated me into the wonderful world of flight with straight and level flying, climbs and glides, turns....a general orientation. What I remember most vividly about that marvelous experience was that, as we cruised over the south suburbs, Bob pointed out landmarks like the racetrack at Washington Park and other prominent features. I was seated in the front, Bob in the back. My hands were not on the stick, and sometimes Bob had both hands on my shoulders. The J-5A flew straight and level as I wondered, "If I'm not flying this airplane, and Bob is not flying this airplane, who is?" It was his way of demonstrating that this little airplane could fly itself better than I could!

I returned the next day for my second lesson and was met by Wilbur who ran the flight school; Wilbur told me that Bob was not available to fly with me and that he, Wilbur, would be my instruction. I was disappointed at this news, but since I was so anxious to fly again, I agreed to settle for Wilbur.

Different instructor, different airplane! But at least I was flying! There were four or five J-5As in Wilbur's fleet, all with 90-hp engines. I guess they all flew about the same but at this point in my training, I couldn't feel any differences.

After a brief pre-flight, I climbed into the front seat of the aircraft and Wilbur spun the prop while standing along side the cabin. He had showed me how to hold the heel brakes that never seemed to work. As he climbed into the rear seat, he asked me if I objected to his "salty" language. After being in Army service and three years as a Railway Postal Clerk, I had heard just about everything, so I said "No!"

J-5As were very noisy and Wilbur had to shout his instructions. After lining up for takeoff he left me no doubt what I was supposed to do next for he yelled in my ear, "Kick'er in the A__!" And that was the beginning of a fun-filled hour of takeoffs and landings, spiced by Wilbur's colorful commands.

About a week later, I returned to fly with Wilbur in yet a different J-5A—more takeoffs and landings.

Two weeks later, I was happy to fly the same airplane in which I had made my first flight, but now I was given Al as my instructor.

Al was not as loud, nor as "salty" as Wilbur, nor was he as daring as Bob. He did scare me once though when we were doing power-off stalls at altitude and I was slow to recover he shouted, "You just crashed!" I evened things up later on when I unwittingly taxied across the end of an active runway just as another airplane zipped in over our heads. Al screamed, "What are you doing? Are you trying to kill me???"

After that, we quit trying to frighten each other and our relationship simmered down to the point where I made real progress toward taming that tail dragger.

On a beautiful late afternoon in October, Al climbed out of that backseat and told me to take it around myself. As I cruised around the pattern that first time, all alone, the thought came to me that comes to many student pilots during their first solo, that is, "What in the world am I doing up here?"

I made three pretty good takeoffs and landings to a full stop. Al shook my hand but he was probably secretly wishing that I would take dancing lessons instead of flying lessons.

One evening, about two weeks later, I went for my first check-ride after solo, in a different J-5A with an instructor I didn't know. I took Wilbur's word that this guy knew what he was doing. We flew one trip around the patch and then he got out of the airplane, leaving me with a "Have fun!"

But this was not my evening for fun because there were five or six airplanes in the pattern and it seemed very crowded and chaotic to a timid fledgling like me. I had trouble getting lined up for takeoff because there was always an airplane coming in short final. As I sat and pondered how to safely get into the traffic flow, some braver or nuttier pilot would jump in ahead of me. (No radios, no way to communicate with each other!)

Eventually, I made three circuits of the field to full-stop landings. Then, as I was waiting my turn to take off again, two J-5As almost collided when one aircraft came within a few feet of landing on top of a plane taking off. That was enough for me! I taxied back to the tie-down and bid Wilbur "Goodbye!!" I wanted to fly—but not like that!

A year passed. Then, one day I heard from my father-in-law, Fred, that an old friend of his was the Fixed Base Operator (FBO) at the Knox, Indiana Airport. About a two-hour drive on a Sunday brought us to Knox where we found the single strip paved runway and an ex-Navy pilot, George, giving instructions in a Cessna 150.

George was quiet and laid-back compared with my previous instructors. He even gave Lois a lesson in which he feigned taking a nap while she flew that 150 straight and level at five thousand feet! Nothing seemed to ruffle his feathers. Only a flagrant mistake on my part brought a simple and direct response from George. He was great to fly with in that C-150 which was quieter and more comfortable than the J-5A. But two hours each way on weekends was a long way to go.

I flew with George two hours that fall, laid off for the winter, flew three more hours with him in the spring, and then quit flying altogether for twelve years.

All during that long layoff, the desire to learn to fly never left me; I just put it on hold while I attended to other important matters.

Chapter Twelve
The House Next Door

I could not have made it through college without Lois' help. She had been working in downtown Chicago since 1959 at Consolidated Book Publishers whose specialties were bibles and cookbooks. Under the guidance and tutelage of her wonderful boss, Mr. Ed Kula, Lois learned to do the payroll and other important assignments. She didn't earn a large salary, but what she did earn she put away in a savings account.

For some months now, Lois and I had been discussing the prospects of owning some income property, so when the house next door at 29 West 114th Place was put up for sale, we bought it. The selling price was low enough that we could pay cash for it, and our neighbor across the street, Attorney Joe Bonifitto, handled the legal matters for a very small fee.

The previous owner was an elderly Italian couple, Mr. and Mrs. Charles Deiro. When Mrs. Deiro passed away, and then very soon after, Mr. Deiro joined her on the other side, their family decided to sell the house because it was quite old and needed a lot of work. This is where we came in.

The house sat on a fifty-by-two-hundred-feet lot, with a side drive and a rather dilapidated three-car garage in the rear. It was a one-story, six-room bungalow, asbestos siding, enclosed front and rear porches. It had a nice firm foundation and a full basement with a dry cement floor throughout. As with many older homes built before the turn of the century, (1900, that is) the layout had a large front room, a large dining room, and a large kitchen; the bedrooms off each of these rooms were very small, with tiny closets (no doors on the closets!). It had only one bathroom that had an antiquated tub and lavatory. One good feature of the house was the heating system. A gas furnace had been installed only a few years earlier, so the house could be kept comfortable in cold weather for a few dollars.

We closed the deal in August 1964, when I was still on summer vacation, so I had plenty of time to start the rehab project. My first target was the plumbing and fixtures in the bathroom.

You must understand that I was a real "greenhorn" at this time in my life, at most everything, especially plumbing. I needed help, and lots of it. Brother-in-law Charlie La Roche was knowledgeable about plumbing and he gave me some good advice: check in at Domby's Hardware down on West 115th

Street, tell them what you are trying to do, and they will help
you do it.

Good Advice!

The bathtub was one of these old cast iron models set up on
four ornamental legs. What goes around comes around. Today,
that tub would cost a fortune and would be considered to be an
antique! But then, I decided to remove it and replace it with a
modern steel tub that rested flat on the floor. Lady Luck smiled
on me for on a trip to the local junkyard on State St. I found a
beautiful, white steel tub that set me back the grand total of $15!

Once I got it into the bathroom, I was faced with the
monumental task of installing it; this is where Domby's
Hardware slid into the picture. The boys at Domby's took me
step-by-step, piece-by-piece, through the installation: new tub
faucet, piping for the shower, drainage supplies, etc. One good
advantage of working like this in a one-story cottage is that the
supply and drain pipes went right through the floor and were
readily accessible in the basement.

I set up a pipe vise, which Fred and Louise let me borrow. In
addition, they introduced me to their set of pipe dies that could
cut and thread any size pipe up to two inches in diameter. That
equipment, the pipe vise and the die set, were lifesavers!

The bathroom sink was a round white bowl with brass
faucets (more antiques that I foolishly discarded!). I put in its
place a modern lavatory with a new medicine cabinet above.

Last, but not least, I removed the old toilet and installed a modern bowl with an up-to-date flush valve. At last, I was Master of that mysterious toilet tank.

In the basement, my pipes looked like a Rube Goldberg contraption, going every which way, but most importantly, they did not leak!

After the plumbing work was finished, getting the house ready to rent was not a major project; it was mostly a matter of cleaning up the rest of the house, doing some painting, and carrying out trash that had accumulated for many years in the basement and in the garage. The furnace was gas generated in good working order and although the house had seen its best days many years in the past, it was reasonably tight for its age. It was warm and comfortable on the coldest days.

When we bought this house, Lois and I had decided not to resell it, but to rent it out for a while as we tried to build up our savings. Now, we needed a tenant and we didn't have to look very far. One of our nieces, Carolyn and her husband, Herb, and their little boy, Herbie, were looking for a place to live, so we rented 29 West to them. It was good that we were able to help Carolyn and her family by giving them a nice, clean, warm place in which to live at a very low rent. Having them right next door meant a lot to her parents and grandparents. And if they had a problem with the house, I was right there to fix it.

They stayed for five years and probably would have stayed longer had not Herb's government job transferred him to Seattle, Washington.

Our next tenant was a young couple with a small child. They stayed two years and then bought a house of their own.

Meanwhile, our neighborhood was changing fast. It seemed like almost overnight, whole blocks in Roseland were going from white to black. On our block, most of the old timers swore up and down that they would not move, but that was just talk. The first one to go was, of all people, our lawyer, Joe Bonifitto.

When 29 West became empty in 1972, we knew that we had to sell it. In order to sell the house, it had to pass inspection by the City of Chicago. On his first inspection, the obese man from the Building Department, told me that I had to replace the sash cords in all the windows; that I had to install new hardware on all the windows; that I had to install doors on the closets and shellac them; all this I did.

On his second visit, this obese gent inspector, who must have weighed in at about 300 pounds, started to jump up and down on the kitchen floor and yelling out that the floor needed to be reinforced! As I stood there viewing this spectacle, I was tempted to reinforce his head with the hammer I held in my hand! We were at his mercy, so I went out and bought a couple of steel posts and installed them in the basement.

On his third visit, he finally passed 29 West. In less than two weeks, we sold the house for almost twice what we paid for it.

Chapter Thirteen
Our House—33 W. 114th Place

As the old saying goes, "Time flies when you're having fun!" Well, while we were not exactly having "fun," all of our lives at 33 West were filled with much joy and laughter and love. It seemed like the 50's and 60's just flew by in no time at all.

You will remember that our "big house" was a four flat; that Lois and I lived downstairs in the rear apartment; that Lois' older sister, Florence ("Tootie") lived in the front apartment with Johnny Rezes, her husband, and his little daughter, Carolyn; Fred and Louise occupied the front apartment upstairs with Lois' younger sister, Ethel ("Tuppie). When Ethel married Charlie La Roche, Ronnie Wieck and his family, who had lived upstairs in the rear for many years, had to move to make room for Ma and Pa Bross, who so generously agreed to give up their spacious five rooms in front to squeeze into the small apartment in the rear—all for Ethel and Charlie! How's that for unselfish parents!

It turned out to be a good move; when in a short time, Charlie and Ethel became the proud parents of a baby girl, Alison.

And so we all grew and prospered throughout the "fabulous 50's" and well into the "sensational 60's."

It was by no means a perfect extended family situation: we all had our little spats and arguments. Living that close to one another, we could hear quite well when tempers heated and boiled over into vociferous shouting matches. We all had a little growing up to do under the watchful eyes of Fred and Louise—Pa and Ma Bross.

Having their three married daughters living in the same building would seem to present to the Brosses a tempting situation where they might interfere or try to control what was happening. But I must say that both Fred and Louise demonstrated marvelous restraint in dealing with our varied problems. For the most part, they minded their own business— and advised each of us to do the same.

Good Advice!

But our pleasant, little family island could not go on forever. All around us, in the late sixties, our neighborhoods were in a state of violent flux. Down on Michigan Avenue in Roseland's old, well-established shopping area, many stores that had been there for years moved out to the suburbs. The handwriting was on the wall.

We had to face the facts no matter how sad they may be. It was especially tough for Fred and Louise to think about leaving this big, old beloved building that they had transformed into our well-loved homes. They, along with many of the other old folks who had to leave their homes in Roseland, seemed to leave a good part of themselves behind in the old neighborhood.

But they were determined that, whatever happened in the impending move, they would try, at all costs, to keep their brood together. So Lois and I, Ethel and Charlie began to search the south suburbs for an apartment building that could possibly become our new home.

While all this was occupying our attention, fate crept into our midst and delivered a stunning blow to the heart of our family. During the summer of 1971, Lois' older sister, Florence, called "Tootie," by the family, began to suffer some aches and pains throughout her body, but mostly in her legs and feet. Johnny took her to the family doctor who diagnosed the problem as a form of arthritis.

No big deal, or so we thought. Tootie had never been a strong girl all of her past life. After she married Johnny, she helped him raise his baby daughter, Carolyn, and then, later on, Tootie spent a lot of time babysitting Ethel's little girl, Alison. Tootie never worked outside her house. She liked to sit on the swing in the backyard and look after her charges or just enjoy the sunshine. She was a happy, contented person.

Her illness continued and gradually, through the months

that followed, got worse. Johnny did not seem to be worried about her for he concluded that the doctor knew what he was doing and that arthritis was difficult to treat. No second opinion was considered.

Finally, in early December 1971, Tootie got so bad that they admitted her into South Shore Hospital. Whatever they did for her there did not help her. Her condition worsened. On Saturday evening, December 18, Lois and I joined Fred and Louise and Johnny at Tootie's bedside. She was dying right there before our eyes and we couldn't believe it. I asked Louise if Tootie had ever been baptized and she said she wasn't sure, so with her permission and Johnny's, I conditionally baptized her. Shortly thereafter, she passed away in peace; her pain was over. Unbelievable!

Some days later, using a plug taken from Tootie's leg as a specimen, it was proved that her cause of death was trichinosis, a disease caused by eating uncooked pork. Her doctors had completely missed the diagnosis.

Tootie's wake and funeral left us all devastated, but especially, her Mom and Dad. They had to bury their first-born child, which is probably the most terrible of all losses; they never got over the pain of her passing—to their dying day.

Our search for a suitable building in the south suburbs was unsuccessful. In general, most of the construction was shabby and the prices would knock your hat off! But what we did find was a nice vacant lot in an area of new construction of apartment buildings in Calumet City. We checked out the builder and were pleasantly surprised to learn that he would provide us with a quality three-flat for a modest sum. Fred and Louise very generously agreed to apply the proceeds from the sale of 33 West as the down payment for our new house—we kids would make the payments on the mortgage.

After Tootie died, Johnny moved out west to live near his daughter, Carolyn. So that meant that our new building could be a three flat. Calhoun Builders showed us some very nice plans for a three flat that had a five-room garden apartment and two six-room apartments upstairs. This layout looked to be just what our family needed, so we signed the purchase agreement and anxiously awaited construction to begin.

Meanwhile, Lois and I were looking for some income property to invest in. Brother Bob was doing quite well with his buildings in Oak Park, Illinois and he encouraged us to take the plunge. We were already fledgling landlords with our rental property at 29 West. But that was only a single-family unit.

Sometime before, I had read William Nickerson's book, *How I Made $1,000 into Five Million Dollars in Real Estate— In My Spare Time.* This book made a lot of sense as the author demonstrated, step-by-step: how to locate, buy, fix-up, and sell income property. If you were willing to do most of the work yourself and to accept the problems that come with being an involved landlord, there was money to be made. I was anxious to try out Mr. Nickerson's methods to see if they really worked. And we didn't have long to wait before we dove into real estate head over heels.

Chapter Fourteen

Knox Apartments, Oak Forest, Illinois

In the spring of 1971, Bob Magrady told us about an ad that had been appearing in the *Chicago Tribune* for many months. It was for thirty-two apartments in Oak Forest, Illinois. Bob said that it looked like a good deal and that we should check it out; he was not interested because he had his hands full with his property in Oak Park. So, one evening, Lois and I drove out to Oak Forest to have a look.

Two blocks east of Cicero Avenue on 153rd Street we found the subjects of this ad—two California-style apartment buildings that were part of a six-building complex. Each two-story brick building held sixteen apartments—eight on each floor which included four one-bedroom units and four studio apartments.

The location was good and the buildings were only fifteen years old. The present owner was a heating and cooling subcontractor who provided the wall furnaces in the original construction. He was very busy handling his own business so he didn't have much time to give to the management and maintenance of the two buildings. He was extremely anxious to unload them.

Fred and Louise took a ride out to Oak Forest to look over the buildings and they were not happy with what they saw. They called the complex "Shanty Town" which was not exactly what Lois and I wanted to hear. Of course, I didn't agree with their appraisal and Lois didn't, either.

We had a lot to think about. It would be a huge step going from being the landlord of a single-family home to becoming owners of two large buildings—thirty-two units in all. It would be a tremendous amount of work. Could we handle the challenge? And what about the financing?

I checked with the real estate agent handling the parcel and when he laid out the facts and figures, I felt that this was too good a deal to pass up. They were only asking $190,000 for both buildings, with a down payment of $25,000; the first mortgage would be $150,000 for twenty years and a balloon mortgage down the line would take care of the rest. We might be able to scrape up the down payment, but when I thought about that BIG mortgage, my knees began to shake!

I guess there is always some trepidation when you're about

to make a big purchase. But my fears were somewhat relieved when I considered Mr. Nickerson's basic premise in his book; you make the down payment on income property, but your tenants will make the payments on the mortgage.

We decided to take the plunge! Mr. Nickerson advised against buying income property if you had to borrow the down payment—that kind of investment usually ended in failure. Somehow, we managed to scrape up the down payment without borrowing. At least from that perspective, we were off to a solid beginning. Now to take a closer look at what we bought.

When we took over the apartments in mid-June 1971, there was no office on the premises. The previous owner handed over two large sets of keys—duplicate to each apartment—and a pack of three-by-five index cards on which were noted the information concerning each tenant. Four or five of the apartments were vacant, so we checked them out first to see if they were up to Lois' standards. We decided not to use one of the studio apartments as an office—we would try to rent all thirty-two units. My briefcase became our traveling office.

Since I was out of school for the summer, I could spend all day there working. Lois could come to help after work and on Saturday and Sunday. And there was plenty to do.

Our plan was to let the tenants know that we were the new owners and that we would be there to fix any problems and to collect their rent. A few complaints emerged from our initial contacts; most of those were leaky faucets or running toilets.

The previous owner was kind enough to show me how to rebuild a faucet and how to replace valves in the toilets. My education in building maintenance had begun!

That first summer learning how to protect our investment was a revelation. Getting to know our tenants was a huge chore. Most of them were good people who were willing to take care of their units and to pay their rent on time, but a few were living like pigs and needed some instructions on how to keep up their living quarters.

One lesson that I quickly learned was how to size up prospective tenants by giving their car a good examination. During our first week in Oak Forest, a young couple pulled into our parking lot, looking for a place to live. They had a small baby with them and their car was a mess! Lois and I had decided that because we only had one bedroom and efficiency apartments to rent that we would not accept children or pets. But I felt sorry for them and let them move into one of our efficiency units on the second floor.

What a horrendous mistake on my part! Within a week, this husband and wife had a big battle and, in a drunken rage, he dismantled the in-wall Murphy bed and threw it over the porch railing out into the yard! Also, one of the wife's visitors a young girl, marked up the wall by the bed with crayons! What a bunch!!

Needless to say, I evicted them at once.

To fill our vacancies, I ran ads in the local newspaper. I

described what was available and gave my home phone number. When some one called, I would screen them in a general way, and then if our needs matched, I would make an appointment to meet at the buildings, usually in the evening or on Saturday or Sunday. Most of the time, the caller would show up, but not always—I made many trips to Oak Forest for nothing.

The apartments, in general, were not in bad shape. We cleaned up the empty ones first by painting, or installing new carpet, and by fixing whatever was broken. One memorable kitchen stove was so filthy that it took Lois *eight* (8) hours to clean it!

When we took over, Oak Forest had well water, which left a deep brown stain on the toilets and bathtubs. To remove these stains was a real challenge. We found that the best remover was muriatic acid—which we used by the gallon. Later on, when Oak Forest got Chicago water, we all celebrated!

For the first two or three years as new income property owners and managers, Lois and I did almost all the work ourselves. We found that dealing with inanimate maintenance problems was much easier to handle than to oversee the sometime bazaar behavior of live tenants. We had to cull a few misfits from our list almost immediately. One single mom's teenage son liked to take target practice in the basement firing at glass bottles—broken glass all over the place! Goodbye!

Another young husband seemed to be okay as long as his

wife was around. As soon as she became sick and went to the hospital, this guy fashioned a small pipe bomb and blew it up late one Saturday night on the building's backstairs— wrecked a few stairs and burned his hand so bad that he ended up in the Emergency Room!

Learning to screen our prospective tenants was a real challenge. Sixteen of our apartments were efficiencies and sixteen were one-bedroom units, so we were limited as to whom we could rent. Our "no children" and "no pet" rules seemed to make sense—the apartments were simply too small for either. One of our older stable tenants was a retired lady who had a cat. She kept her place clean and paid her rent on time, so "kitty" became invisible.

The lawns in front of the buildings were large and needed servicing. I cut the grass myself for the first couple summers with a walk-behind power mower. Then, we picked up a second-hand riding mower with a worn out engine. From Sears, we bought a new engine and Mike Kurasz and my nephew, Charlie Fox, installed it on our mower. They did a nice job and the mower ran just fine, so I bought a special hardened chain to lock the mower under one of the building's stairs. Special lock, too! But one dark night, someone sawed off the lock and chain and stole the mower! Never saw it again!

The months and years passed. Lois and I still had our regular jobs to go to and yet we were managing and maintaining 32 apartments. We needed help. And help we got from my nephew, Charlie Fox.

Charlie had a wife, Joan, and a son and daughter, lived in Chicago's Hegewisch neighborhood. He worked as an accountant during the week, but on Saturdays, he became my "right-hand man." Charlie was a good painter and a good plumber. Together we fixed every problem that came along. Having him with me on Saturdays helped to lessen some of the stress that threatened to botch our combined efforts. Lois could now remain at home to take care of our own house and family. Charlie enjoyed working at the buildings and he even envisioned that someday he might own some income property himself.

But it was not to be.

Chapter Fifteen
Farewell, Fred & Louise!

By the second week of November 1972, Fred and Louise had sold our beloved home at 33 West and we were preparing to move into our newly completed three-flat on Memorial Drive in Calumet City, Illinois.

You can imagine what a tremendous undertaking this move would be because of the many years that the Brosses and the rest of the family had occupied these premises. For Lois and me packing up our belongings in our three-and-a-half rooms was not bad at all. But it was the basement and the garage and the chicken coup in the backyard that presented the real challenges.

During their long years together Fred and Louise had accumulated all sorts of tools, hardware, odds and ends, "you name it" that was stored mostly in the basement, but some in the garage. Our new house in Calumet City had no basement but just a small furnace room for storage. So we could not take everything with us, but had to leave much behind for the new tenants. Deciding what to take and what to leave became a very painful process. A few days before we moved, we held a "garage sale" to try to get rid of a lot of our stuff, but we ended up giving most of it away to our new neighbors.

Jensen Movers did the actual moving for us—a back-braking, all-day job at that. By the evening of November 11, we were all safe and sound in our new quarters—Lois and I upstairs in the second floor apartment, Ethel and Charlie in the first floor apartment, and Fred and Louise downstairs in the Garden Apartment.

Leaving 33 West forever left us all emotionally drained, but especially Fred and Louise. As I said before, when the old folks were forced to leave their beloved home in which they had spent so many happy years, they left a part of themselves back in the "ole neighborhood." Fred and Louise Bross were no different—this move just about killed them!

But life must go on! For Lois and me and for Ethel and Charlie our sadness in leaving Roseland was tempered by the joy we felt in setting up and furnishing our new apartments. We had so much more room now and it was fun to play at interior decorating. We still had our regular jobs to go to and the buildings in Oak Forest to take care of, and now this swell new home in Calumet City to enjoy. The future began to look brighter!

Our move to Calumet City brought me a lot closer to my teaching job at Edison School in Hammond; it only took me about ten minutes to drive to school. But for Lois and Charlie La Roche, who both worked in down town Chicago, getting to work meant a much longer ride. Lois drove the Dan Ryan Expressway every weekday for sixteen years, while Charlie rode a bus to his job most of the time. I don't know how Lois put up with such a stressful drive. Having a beautiful little golden 1973 Camaro sport coupe, which faithfully carried her down town and home again each day, helped to lessen the strain of her commute.

As time passed, Lois and I, and Ethel and Charlie became better adjusted in our new home. Not so with Fred and Louise downstairs in their Garden Apartment. Their place was damp and difficult to heat well. They sacrificed (once again!) their own comfort to give their daughters much better accommodations upstairs. After working their whole lives to buy, renovate, and maintain 33 West, they had to leave it and to sell it on government terms! This was enough to suck the life out of anyone, and as the days passed, you could see first Fred, and then Louise, began to go downhill.

After Fred had retired in 1963, his health had never been the greatest. He was functioning on only one kidney and he had a spot on his lung. In the spring of 1974, Fred was ailing, so he, being a veteran of World War I, checked into Hines Hospital in

Maywood, Illinois, where he had received successful treatment in the past.

We visited him there and did not think that his condition was critical. But a few days later, Fred died suddenly at 9:15 A.M. on May 8, 1974. The cause of death was listed as chronic renal failure and diabetes mellitus. We waked him at Doty-Panozzo Funeral Home on 115th Street in the old neighborhood. No fancy suit for Fred's departure—we laid him out in his pale blue pajamas, fitting vesture for his Big Sleep in Cedar Park Cemetery alongside his beloved daughter, Florence.

Once again our whole house was in mourning. Louise took Fred's passing pretty well. Lois had been very close to her father, so this was very tough on her. I tried to help her as much as I could but each person has to grieve in his or her own way. It takes time to get over the pain and the loss, but in this case, we were not given the time we needed for in just two months after Fred's passing, Louise suffered a massive stroke!

She was not one to complain, so one afternoon, when Louise did say how badly she felt, Lois drove her over to Dr. William Smith's office on Commercial Avenue in South Chicago. When Dr. Smith examined Louise, he told Lois to immediately take her over to be admitted to the Emergency Room at South Shore Hospital.

From the ER, they sent her to Intensive Care where they treated her for heart failure and resulting edema in her lungs. After a couple of days, Louise's condition seemed to be improving, so they transferred her to a regular two-bed room. That very night she suffered a massive stroke that her nurses did not become aware of until the following morning.

Sadly, from that time on, Louise could no longer communicate with Lois and Ethel, who had been with her constantly since her admission. For days they spoon fed her and attended to her special needs, as her life's vitality slowly ebbed away. Then, one afternoon, the end came as Louise Bross peacefully passed away. That great heart of the Bross Family had finally stopped beating.

Louise joined Fred and Florence in Cedar Park Cemetery; she was buried on Fred's birthday, July 31, 1974.

Chapter Sixteen

A Pilot, at Last!

Life goes on! Soon after Louise's passing, Ethel and Charlie and Lois and I took a trip up north to the Woods to perform some needed maintenance on the house and to get our minds off the sadness that hung over our family. We usually didn't go up there together, but this was a special time in our lives and Louise's death seemed to bring us all closer together. I guess, in our minds, we were determined to do something nice for Ma and Pa Bross so we grabbed rollers and paint brushes and put a beautiful new coat of paint on the exterior of the house and garage—even the fish house, too!

We had a good time for a week or so, even with the hard work and, as usual, the days flew by and our responsibilities back home necessitated our return—Charlie and Lois to their jobs and me to the buildings in Oak Forest.

That long ride of 9 to 10 hours back home reminded me

again of why I wanted to learn to fly. That old aviation bug began to stir up new dreams.

It had been twelve years since I had flown an airplane. All during that long layoff, the desire to learn to fly never left me. Finally, in July 1975, I returned to the Lansing, Illinois Airport.

In the interval, things had changed. The east-west runway was now paved, but the north-south runway was still sod. One flight school had high-winged Cessnas and the other had low-winged Piper Cherokee 140's that caught my fancy. I went back to the Pipers and have never been sorry.

A young lad named Randy was assigned to be my instructor, and that was my lucky day. But after the long layoff, it was like starting all over again.

From the very beginning, working with Randy showed me what had been lacking in my previous instructors. With George, and Wilbur, and Al, for the most part, we just got into the airplane and went flying. Not so with Randy.

Before I ever got inside the Piper PA28-140, he took me on a familiarization walk around that airplane that had me looking closely at hinges and flaps, moving ailerons, checking the oil dip stick and spark plug connections under the cowl, running my fingers along the edge of the propeller to feel for nicks, draining the sumps, looking into the gas tanks and at other important items that made up the logical inspection of the airplane that we call the "preflight."

In the air, Randy was just as thorough as he was on the

ground. He watched my every move, making corrections when needed, but otherwise he was quiet and reserved.

He brought me along in an organized fashion. As a teacher, I knew that he must be following a lesson plan because, when we flew every four or five days or at least once a week, he didn't have to ask, "What did we do last time?" When we worked on forced landings and emergency procedures, for example, Randy started the next lesson with a thorough review of how to get down safely—every lesson started with a review of the last flight.

And the only time Randy missed an appointment with me was the day when his boss, Joe Herron, sent him on an emergency charter flight. Then Joe took over for him and flew with me (an important check ride preceding my first supervised solo in the Cherokee). But that was the only time that Randy was not present and prepared.

Since I had soloed the Piper J-5 some years earlier, taking the Cherokee up alone was not a completely new experience. But still I was nervous and apprehensive that I might foul up somehow. I guess it's normal that most fledgling pilots have some sort of jitters before their solo flights. Once aloft, their training gives them the confidence to be successful in their maneuvers.

I made three good takeoffs and landings to a full stop. I was elated!! Now, on to the next step!

Airplanes are primarily meant for going somewhere. Once I

learned to control the airplane and to do basic maneuvers at the airport or nearby in a practice area, I was ready to move from this "local" flying to preparing for my first cross-country flight.

Before a pilot ever takes off on a cross country, he is required to learn all he can about conditions at the intended destination airport, to check the weather in route and at this landing site, to know about anything that might jeopardize the safety of the flight.

Randy had me prepare a flight plan for a flight from Lansing, IL to South Bend, IN—a distance of about 80 miles, almost due east.

We took off, climbed to three thousand feet and flew east on a heading of 85°. The weather was clear and Lake Michigan's shore beckoned to me as we cruised along. For some reason or another, instead of closely following my heading, I was fascinated by the gorgeous view out of my left window and, without realizing it, I was following the curvature of the lake's shoreline.

Randy let me fly on for a little bit, and then he said, "I thought we were going to South Bend!" I snapped out of my lethargy and returned to the true course.

The higher you go in an airplane, the sense of speed diminishes, but you are still moving right along and trying to pick out checkpoints on the ground that are shown on the aeronautical chart on your clipboard. This is not easy. You have to fly the airplane, keep your altitude and heading, and locate your checkpoints. It takes a lot of practice.

Before I realized it, we were approaching South Bend and Randy made a radio call to Air Traffic Control to get permission to fly in their airspace. He guided us into the landing pattern and I was so excited that I forgot to lower our landing flaps as we came in on a long final. Well, I got the flaps down and made a decent landing, taxied over to the terminal and shut down the engine.

"Whew! That was great!"

We had a cup of coffee in the terminal and then headed back home. A total of one hour and forty-two minutes in the air for the round trip! The same trip by car could take, at least five or six hours. Next week, we would fly a longer route to Fort Wayne, IN.

Three weeks passed before I was able to fly again. These long intervals of inactivity tended to impede my progress, but they were unavoidable. I planned and flew the round trip to Fort Wayne with Randy giving me a good workout in pilotage (visually identifying prominent features on the ground with symbols on my chart), VDR navigation, lost procedures, and dead reckoning. This time we covered the 280 miles in three hours and six minutes. Cherokee 140's are not noted for their speed (cruise about 105 mph) but they are excellent trainers, easy to fly, and very safe. It is often said that the most dangerous aspect of flying is the auto trip to the airport!

Schoolwork and work at our buildings kept me from flying as often as I would have liked. But, eventually, at about weekly intervals, I was able to make another trip to South Bend and then a trip to Champaign, IL. Little-by-little, trip-by-trip, I was gaining experience and building confidence in myself and in the airplanes that I flew.

At the beginning, Randy handled the radio chores while I was busy keeping the airplane right side up. But now, he got me more involved in communicating with Air Traffic Control and with pilots in other aircraft. The Cardinal Rule in Aviation is: Aviate, Navigate, Communicate—in that order; a pilot must keep his priorities in line if he is to stay out of trouble.

I suppose that I was no more timid on the radio than most other beginning airmen, but I must admit the whole process scared me more than the actual flying. Once I realized that controllers are pilots' best friends, the tension that I felt on the mike began to subside. I didn't know it at the time, my learning was less than normal and this, along with radios that were not real clear, gave me fits.

Another huge hurdle lay in my path. I had plenty of hours flying around the pattern at Lansing (I was almost like the guy who had 500 hours, but never left the pattern!), many hours doing maneuvers in the practice areas nearby, a few hours flying cross country with Randy at my side—but now I had to leave the comfort of familiar landscapes and proceed into the unknown—all alone—solo!!

I planned a cross country to Champaign, IL and when I took off, my knees were shaking and my feet were trembling on the rudder pedals. About twenty miles out of Champaign, their controller could tell by my shaky voice, "here comes another one of those nervous student pilots!" Anyway, he guided me on down I-57 to the airport, where I made a decent landing and had him sign my logbook. The trip back home was a snap compared with the outbound fiasco.

During the next couple of weeks, I made solo cross-country flights down to Lafayette, IN and to Danville, IL. Then, as required by the licensing statutes, I flew solo from Lansing, IL to Springfield, IL, then on to Moline, IL, and then back home to Lansing—a total flight time of 4 hours and 42 minutes.

The next required item for the private pilot's license was three hours of night flight. When I took off that first time in complete darkness, Randy helped me to overcome my nervousness as we flew around the pattern, which by now had become very familiar. He said, "The airplane doesn't know its night!" The lights along the runway and the lights scattered nearby in the area, presented to us a panorama that was startlingly beautiful!

We practiced takeoffs and landings, then left the airport area to work on VDR navigation, pilotage, and forced landings.

Flying at night is a whole different ball game. It is much more difficult than flying during the day. After dark, it is very easy to fly into clouds that you cannot see and just as easy to fly into those rocky hillsides that seem to reach up to grab the unsuspecting pilot. On very dark, moonless nights, when no outside reference is available, pilots must fly by instruments to keep the aircraft right side up. The FAA requires those three hours at night as a safeguard in case the rookie airman gets caught aloft after the sun sets.

After I completed my solo cross-country flights and flew those three hours at night, Randy began a series of reviews of all the basic maneuvers of flight. I had passed the written portion of the exam for Private Pilot some months earlier.

At last, after some seventy hours in my logbook, Randy made the entry that I was waiting for—he certified me ready for the flight test!

A few days later, I met with the FAA Flight Examiner, Robert Lakin, at Lansing Airport. This was a stunning coincidence in that this man who would evaluate my flying abilities was none other than Bob Lakin who had given me my first lesson in that Piper J-5 some sixteen years earlier!

I don't know if Bob remembered me or not. We sat at a desk and went over a few basics in navigation and then he had me plan a short cross-country trip to Rockford, Illinois and then we went flying. Before we departed Lansing, Bob had me do some crosswind landings on Runway 27; the wind was about 15 mph out of 180° so this was a good test of my crosswind technique. Not real good—but passable.

On the way to Rockford, Bob demonstrated using a DF Steer

when you were lost. He could see that I could hold my altitude and heading, so he had me land at Clow International Airport where the runway is north and south—easy landing there.

After we landed back at Lansing, Bob said, "I've seen better, but I've seen worse. You have passed your flight test. Congratulations!" The date was June 17, 1976.

A few weeks later, Randy had a disagreement with his boss and quit the flying school. I was devastated! But the boss assured me that Randy's replacement was an excellent instructor and that I would not be disappointed. I looked forward to continuing my work toward the instrument rating with my new man, Bruce.

But my new man, Bruce, was an old man—quite the opposite of Randy in years, but like him in his meticulous approach to the preflight and other details of flight. And flying with Bruce proved to be the very best time of my life in the air.

Bruce was a pioneer pilot. He caught Lindbergh's spirit and built his own Swallow and learned to fly it in the early thirties. When World War II came along, Bruce was already too old to fly for the U.S. Army Air Corps, but he did more than his part by ferrying thirty-nine bombers across the Atlantic Ocean to England.

After the war, Bruce bought a half-interest in a P-51 Mustang and raced it to victory in the Cleveland Air Races. He flew charter and instructed for many years and appeared in air shows. He was a "real" pilot.

Here I was, a rookie airplane driver, trying to learn something from the "old Pro." With every lesson I discovered a little more of how to fly an airplane. We both knew that my abilities were limited, but Bruce shared his vast knowledge with me as if I were a young astronaut in training, instead of me being a middle-aged pretender.

But the instrument ticket was beyond my reach. I know that I hurt Bruce's feelings when I failed the instrument flight test twice. After that, he suggested that I forget about it, and "Let's just fly for fun!"

That's what we did for several years, as we became fast friends. Then Bruce's health failed. As he lay dying in the hospital, he told me "Charlie, if I knew that it was going to be like this, I would much rather have "spun in!"

Chapter Seventeen
Gains and Losses!

All the time while I was working toward my Private Pilot's License, I was continuing to give my all at school and at the buildings in Oak Forest. Each New Year in the classroom presented more problems and far less satisfaction than I had experienced in the early years. I was looking forward toward an early retirement. My stomach pains and stress headaches were returning—similar to the ones that resulted in my ulcer surgery in the spring of 1972, where I lost two-thirds of my stomach: I didn't want to go through that again.

At the buildings, Lois and I were still doing all of the work, with little outside help. We tried using some of our nieces and nephews to clean and paint the vacant apartments, but that didn't work well at all. Finally, after we struggled for several years, my nephew, Charlie Fox, agreed to help us out on Saturdays.

Charlie Fox was my sister Irene's second oldest boy. He was in his early thirties, married to Joan, and had two children, Charles and Lisa. They owned a nice little brick bungalow in Hegewisch. During the week, Charlie did accounting work, which he didn't like very well. After his days in the office, he enjoyed fixing things around the house, with help from his father-in-law, Mike Kurasz, who was a master craftsman. In his garage, Charlie was restoring an antique automobile—a 1928 Ford Model T Sedan.

Even though Charlie was only available on Saturdays, he was prompt and dependable and he enjoyed doing whatever job I gave him. We worked well together, and in no time at all, Charlie became my right-hand man.

In addition to helping me at the buildings, I discovered that Charlie also was interested in aviation, so after I got my pilot's license, he became my number one passenger. Lois had lost interest in flying with me, especially since I scared her a few times. Sunday morning became the best time for Charlie and me to enjoy a few hours in the air. One of my lady tenants at the buildings had a boyfriend who owned a Cessna 310 twin-engine airplane and he was kind enough to take Charlie and me for a ride.

We flew from the airport in Crestview down around the VDR at Joliet and back. He let me fly the airplane and I made a few turns and flew straight and level—a marvelous experience!

Summer of 1977 turned into fall and then, one fateful Friday night around midnight, our phone rang. It was Charlie Fox's brother-in-law, Sonny, who gave me the bad news straight out—Charlie Fox was dead! Earlier that evening, while working on one of his old cars in his garage, he was overcome by carbon monoxide. He was used to working till late at night on his cars but this night he complained to Joan earlier that he had a headache and just didn't feel well. But in spite of feeling badly, he went out into the garage anyway. He was testing the engine in his old station wagon and he didn't have the garage door open sufficiently to disperse the deadly fumes. Joan found him sitting behind the steering wheel with a wrench in his hand, the motor running and the garage filled with the deadly exhaust fumes. He should have known better!

I have had several near-mortal blows before in my lifetime, but this shocking news was almost more than I could handle. The next day, Saturday, I had to go to the buildings and when I tried to relate the sorrowful news to several of my old tenants, the tears poured shamelessly from my eyes. I could not keep from crying.

Joan and the kids and the whole family were devastated. The wake and funeral left us all basket cases, but we had to help each other to get through this crisis. We each had our own grief to deal with in our own personal way. Our mourning would go on and on and on.

Charlie's death changed all of our lives. He and I had

discussed going in as partners on possible future real estate deals. We had looked at some rental properties that looked good for investments. He knew that there was money to be made in owning income property and he wanted the best for his family, but now the worst had come to pass.

In the months that followed Charlie's passing, my interest in the buildings grew less and less. The old fire was gone—along with my dearly departed nephew! My "right hand" at the buildings was no more and so was my copilot—"Gone West," as they say. Flying would always be in my blood, but I began to think about putting the buildings up for sale.

Back in the classroom in the fall of 1978, the old stresses reappeared. Headaches and stomach problems reminded me of my pre-surgery days of 1972. I was still flying about once a week, which helped to relieve the pressures of teaching and being a landlord.

I knew that I could not go on like this much longer, so I listed the buildings with a realtor. At the time, it probably would have been much wiser to have kept the buildings and have someone else manage them and do the maintenance work, but I wanted the load removed from my shoulders completely, once and for all!

Six months passed with no buyers on the horizon. Then, all at once, when I was ready to take the buildings off the market, three different people made offers and they were even bidding against each other. We had the chance now to make a nice profit on our investment, so, with some trepidation, we closed the deal in January 1979.

A-a-a-ah! What a relief!

For the first time in years, I was able to sleep peacefully without worrying that some silly tenant might wreck havoc on our poor apartments! Things were looking up!

But I still had that teaching albatross around my neck, and when conditions at school went from bad to worse, after carefully figuring out our future financial situation, I threw in the sponge and retired from teaching, once and for all! It was February 1979, and I was fifty-six years old!

Now I had time to get myself straightened out—physically, emotionally, and most importantly, spiritually. While working at Edison School the last few years, I had been able to attend daily Mass at St. Victor's in Calumet City. Receiving Our Lord in Holy Communion every day gave me the strength to battle the many demons that plagued my conscious, and sometimes unconscious, existence. Some battles I won, and some battles I lost, but the war goes on, even to this day.

Now in retirement, I had more time for flying; Bruce kept trying to polish some of the rough spots in my aviating skills. The airplanes we flew were always rented from FTI Aviation at Lansing. I made two trips cross country up to Janesville, Wisconsin and one trip to Lone Rock, Wisconsin. I was still planning to fly all the way up to Rice Lake to our cottage. That was the whole idea in my learning to fly in the first place.

But renting was expensive—especially for long trips. So I began to look around for an airplane that would be suitable for our needs. I pored over many aviation magazines, reading reports about what the used airplane market had to offer. I read an article in a magazine, which gave the Cessna Cardinal a glowing review, and, soon after, in the *Trade-A-Plane* newspaper, I saw a 1970 Cessna Cardinal advertised for sale.

Bruce became my advisor in this matter and he really liked the Cessna Cardinal because he had flown one recently instructing a young lady student pilot. We flew up to Cottonwood Airport outside of Rockford, IL, where the airplane was based, met the young owner-pilot, and went for a ride. I flew in the right seat to a nearby airstrip where the owner let me do some touch-and-goes.

Everything went well, the price was right, Bruce liked the airplane, and so I bought it. The following week, I drove Bruce up to Rockford to close the deal and to pick up the airplane. Bruce flew the Cardinal back to Lansing and now I was the proud owner of my own airplane. Thank You Lord!

The Cardinal was a high-wing monoplane with a 180-hp engine and an adjustable pitch propeller—not much different than the Piper Cherokee that I had been flying. Bruce helped me to become familiar with the airplane, inside and out. Now with my own airplane, I could fly anytime I wished and Bruce was available most of the time, so we began a series of flights to get me checked out in the Cardinal.

Bruce was very thorough and did not rush my training. By now I had just over three hundred hours in my logbook, so I was no raw rookie. In my mind, the Cardinal was a great airplane that could carry Lois and me up to the North Woods in style and comfort. But it was not to be!

After almost eighteen hours flying the Cardinal, one fateful Saturday morning, Bruce let me go solo. My takeoff and flight around the pattern at Lansing were fine and so was my approach to landing on Runway 27—light winds right down the runway. I had it nailed right on seventy miles per hour, full flaps, everything looked great! Then, just as I touched down, the airplane began to pitch up and down like a bucking bronco! I learned later that the nose gear collapsed and the propeller struck the cement runway causing the violet pitching. I was belted in tightly so I was not injured but my pretty new Cardinal was a real mess!

When I bought this airplane, the previous owner told me that the nose gear had been damaged but the repairs made it as good as new. I think that the repair was faulty that led to the nose gear's collapse. A bitter lesson! I should have known better! The Cardinal was totaled and I sold it a few weeks later. I was fortunate that my insurance covered the crash, so I only lost about a thousand dollars for my foolishness!

After the fiasco with the Cardinal, I didn't fly for three months. I guess my confidence in flying airplanes was sorely bruised. My dear Lois, who had been so generous financially in helping me to buy the Cardinal, now took me to task for buying a high-wing Cessna when I had felt so comfortable in the low-wing Pipers. I guess she was right—as she usually is.

I thought for sure that my insurance broker would be upset because I had made that claim so soon after buying the policy, but, au contraire, he was very nice about it and encouraged me to get back "on my mount" as soon as possible!" In a few weeks time, I did "mount up" again, but this time I went back to my beloved Piper Cherokees!

Getting back in the left seat again was not as difficult as I thought; flying the old familiar Cherokees again helped to bolster my confidence, and Bruce was always there to give me his support.

The fall and winter of 79-80 became a dormant period in my love affair with airplanes. But in the spring, this not-so-young man's fancy turned to thoughts of flight! I still dreamed of flying up North, so when Joe Herron, the owner of FTI Flying School where I got my private license, made me an offer I couldn't refuse, I became the proud owner of one of my training airplanes—a 1973 Piper Cherokee PA-28 140 N 56363!

They say, "Don't buy a trainer!" But "363," as I lovingly called her, was in pretty good shape because I knew that Joe kept his airplanes in tip-top condition. His mechanics were guys that I knew and trusted. "363" would be my "gal" for the next three years.

This time, Lois approved of my purchase and we enjoyed

flying over our house in Calumet City and seeing it from 1,500 feet was a real thrill.

In July, we flew up to Janesville, Wisconsin for our "$50 hamburger." It was right on our way up to the Woods and served as a practice run for our long-awaited flight to Rice Lake. Finally, a week or so later, with great flying weather forecast, Lois and I took "363" on her maiden trip to Northern Wisconsin.

Cherokees are not noted for their speed, so a pretty stiff headwind kept our ground speed down to about 90 mph. The visibility was excellent but at our low altitude of 3,000 feet, there was a mild chop in the turbulent air. We stopped to refuel in Lone Rock—about halfway on our trip. There is only one word that can adequately describe the rest of our flight and that is "FANTASTIC!"

The beautiful rolling hills around Eau Claire are lovely to look at through the car windows, but to fly over this gorgeous countryside was a visual treat well worth waiting for. And to fly into Rice Lake for the first time was truly wonderful.

Carl Rindlisbacher, the longtime manager of the Rice Lake Airport, was very gracious on our arrival. He told us we could tie down "363" there, free of charge, as long as we liked.

Carl was a great friend of pilots and he constructed beautiful weather maps to help us with our flight plans. He loved working at the airport; it was his whole life. And, a few years later, when the new airport was built and he was forced to retire, planners named the new airport "Carl's Field" in his honor. He is sorely missed.

We stayed at the cottage for about a week, and then I started to check the weather picture to plan our flight home. We made a couple false starts from the cottage to the Rice Lake Airport because there was a stubborn stationary weather front holding tight over Chicago.

Finally, we departed. The weather down to Lone Rock was great. There we gassed up but I made the mistake of not filling the tanks to the top, but only to the tabs, which took one hour's flying time out of each tank. I did it to save weight, but I would regret it later.

I checked Chicago weather at Lone Rock and it appeared that we would have no problem getting home to Lansing. But as soon as we left Lone Rock the clouds began to increase and lower, along with the visibility. It was still VFR so on we flew.

At Janesville, it was still pretty good, but by the time we reached DuPage Airport, I could no longer see it as we flew past. We only had a few more miles to get home, when it happened! We flew into a wall of rain that the Northeast wind blew off Lake Michigan and wham! Just like that I could see absolutely nothing out of the windshield.

It's a good thing that I had had some instrument training for I carefully put "363" into a shallow turn which took us 180° to head back toward DuPage. Lois was reading the names of towns on the water towers as we flew along above the 294 Expressway at 1,500 feet.

Our gas was running low and I knew that if I couldn't find DuPage, we probably could not make it all the way back to Janesville.

I called Chicago Radio for DF (Direction Finder) Steer, which Bob Lakin had demonstrated for me during my Private Pilot License Test. It would give me a heading to the closest airport. But, to my dismay, the DF equipment that day was not in use. Strike One!

Then, I asked Chicago Radio to check my location from my transponder signal, but they told me that they could not see our blip because our transponder was not working! Strike Two!

Just about then, when things were looking bleakest, the Good Lord took over to give us a helping hand—Lois looked out to the east and spotted the lovely, crisscrossed runways of Midway Airport. We were only about two miles west of the field when I called their tower. Fortunately, on this quiet Sunday afternoon, there was no other traffic, so they gave us clearance to land and land we did!

The boys in the tower chewed me out for not calling in sooner, but when I told them that I was lost, they let it go at that.

We had to unload all our stuff from "363" into a rental car to take us the rest of the way home. To say that Lois was upset with this outcome would be putting it mildly. I took the rental car back the next morning and flew "363" back home to Lansing.

Wouldn't you know it, the weather then was CAVU—ceiling and visibility unlimited!

After this unfortunate bout with the weather, it was extremely difficult for me to justify the utility of a light airplane to my wife, Lois. Later that year she flew with me again several times, but only on shorter, local flights. For reasons I cannot fully explain, I did not attempt to fly up to the Woods again until the following summer, June 1982.

Because she thoroughly disliked that long car ride north, Lois again became my copilot. On this trip, everything went well until we were ready to land on the Rice Lake north-south runway. A very, strong crosswind was howling at 90° from the west across the runway. My crosswind landing technique was never the greatest, so after two unsuccessful attempts to land, for safety reasons, I gave up and flew the ten miles over to Barron, where we landed nicely into the wind on their sod strip. Lois chided me for landing her in a "cornfield!" The flight home was uneventful but it was the last time Lois ever set foot in "363."

As with everything else, the way to learn to do something well is to do it over and over again. With every cross-country flight I made, I learned more and more each time what flying was all about. Two months later, in August 1982, I made a solo trip to the Woods; it would be my last flight up there in "363."

In the months that followed, my flying took on a local flavor—once again, I was almost like the guy who had 500 hours and never left the pattern! My "copilot" had deserted the aircraft, so my reasons for continuing to own my own airplane were disappearing.

With many misgivings, I put "363" up for sale. Again, as with the buildings, at first no one wanted her, then several potential buyers appeared at once. I sold her to two partner-pilots who I knew would give her good care. My long, lost love, Goodbye!!

Chapter Eighteen
Adieu! Adieu!

After I sold my airplane, I didn't fly again for three years. Meanwhile, my dear friend and mentor, Bruce, was ailing. His health was deteriorating quite rapidly and this for a man who had never been sick all his life. The big "C" cancer cut him down. A few months earlier Bruce was flight-testing his "Bug"—a single-seat biplane that he was restoring and when his engine quit on takeoff, he managed to crash land in an adjoining field at Lansing.

I saw him in the ER where the nurses were astonished that the cause of his minor injuries at age 84 was from an airplane crash! After that, Bruce seemed to go downhill fast and I was at St. Margaret's Hospital on the day he died. He had come close to death so many times in his long aviation career, but he always managed to avoid disaster. This time, his number was up.

Bruce and Honey, his wife, had no children. I was privileged to have been one of his pallbearers as we laid him to rest in Elmwood Cemetery, Hammond, Indiana. Maybe when I get to heaven, Bruce will be there, waiting to give me my "WINGS!"

No "363," no Bruce, my thoughts now turned to other things in my retirement. Of course, I still attended daily Mass because it seemed that was the only way I could even come close to doing God's Will. The "war" goes on!

A few days before Christmas 1984, my sister Evie's husband, Ray Adams, died after having heart surgery at Northwestern Hospital. Five years earlier, he had had open-heart surgery at Mercy Hospital, but apparently, the plaque in his arteries built up again. This time he didn't make it. Once again our family was in mourning. Ray was a nice guy and all his family loved him dearly.

In my retirement, along with my flying ambitions, I began to write short stories and articles, mostly about aviation or religion. I thought that I could make some money as a freelance writer, but my success in that field was very limited.

I sold two pieces to aviation magazines—one "Never Again," an account of our bout with the weather over Chicago, and the other was a biographical piece on Bruce. In addition, I sold a short nostalgic piece to a religious magazine in Milwaukee. But that was about it. I have a file drawer full of

unpublished works and rejection slips. Writing is not easy; try
it sometime!

In the summer of 1985, Lois and I were thinking about
getting involved in some kind of volunteer work. Then, one
Sunday, I noticed an ad in my parish bulletin at St. Victor's in
Calumet City. It was a plea for volunteers at St. Margaret
Hospital in North Hammond. This hospital was only ten
minutes away from our house so we called the Volunteer Office
there and set up an interview.

Angie Nagy, the Head of the Volunteer Department, met
with us one afternoon and outlined what volunteering at the
hospital was all about. Her main point was that the work there
would prove to be very rewarding—that the Franciscan
summation "It is in giving, that we receive," would make itself
felt in our hearts and minds. So Lois and I signed up to offer our
services two afternoons a week—a decision we would applaud
for years to come.

After a short training period, Lois and I began our service as
volunteers at St. Margaret's. We worked Wednesday
afternoons—Lois on the sixth floor and I on the fourth floor,
4E—General Surgery. Our assignments put us on duty in the
Nurses' Stations where we ran errands for the nurses and for the
clerks, discharged patients, and generally made ourselves
available to help out any way we could.

On Friday evening, from 5 P.M. to 8 P.M., Lois took charge of the visitors' waiting room on the second floor and I reported to the Nurse-in-Charge in the Emergency Room. As I was pondering over my situation that first memorable Friday evening, the scene in the ER exploded from quiet inaction to one of frantic activity.

Several nurses and ambulance attendants hurriedly wheeled in a young man who had smashed his motorcycle into a car over in Calumet City. He was not breathing.

In just a few moments, the doctors and nurses surrounded his gurney and used every procedure at hand to try to save his life. But their efforts were in vain; he was DOA—Dead on Arrival!

Almost, at once, the lad's mother and girlfriend burst upon the scene and when they learned the horrible news, they screamed and wailed and shrieked up and down the hallway outside of the ER.

I was appalled at this sorrowful scene and I thought to myself that if volunteer duty in the ER is going to be like this, then I don't think I could handle it. But, Thanks to the Good Lord, this terrible experience was a one-time occurrence.

For the next five years, Lois and I spent our Friday evenings working at the hospital, but when they remodeled and enlarged the ER section, we terminated that part of our volunteering. Our work upstairs with Lois in Rehab and me in 4E continued for some twenty-two years in total.

All through the years, Lois and I had remained in close touch with my dear friend, Joe Germanos, and his family. They lived over in Elmwood Park and Joe had his optometry practice and jewelry business downtown Chicago on Washington, near Dearborn. Joe and Jeannine had five kids, so they were mighty busy most of the time. They could not travel out south to our "neck of the woods," so many Friday afternoons, Joe would give me a call and say, "Mac, why don't you and Lois take a ride tomorrow evening." And many a Saturday evening, we did just that.

We had such good times together, just talking or walking around his neighborhood, or, in season, taking a dip in Joe's swimming pool. Oh, the joys of the simple pleasures in life! But they, too, ended all too soon.

Just as in Ray Adams' case, Joe's heart began to give him trouble and for the last two years of his life, his strength and vitality slowly ebbed away. He kept working all this time, and one morning as he was about to unlock his down town office, his heart failed and he died on the spot. His daughter, Debbie, called me on the phone and said, "My father died this morning!" Will we ever be free from these disturbing phone calls!?!

Joe's death ended our trips to Elmwood Park. We still had Evie and Walter and Mary in Oak Park, and Bob and Millie in

Berkeley, but in a few short years, they too, would bid us a final adieu! So here I am, the "Last of the Magradys," looking forward to our grand reunion in Heaven.

May God Bless Us All!! Amen!